Inscriptions

INSCRIPTIONS

A Prairie Poetry Anthology

Dennis Cooley, Editor

Turnstone Press

Turnstone Press
607-100 Arthur Street
Winnipeg, Manitoba
Canada R3B 1H3

Turnstone Press gratefully acknowledges the assistance of the Canada Council and the Manitoba Arts Council.

Cover design: Doowah Design

Text design: Manuela Dias

This book was printed and bound in Canada by Hignell Printing Limited for Turnstone Press.

Canadian Cataloguing in Publication Data

Main entry under title:

Inscriptions: a Prairie poetry anthology

ISBN 0-88801-168-7

1. Canadian poetry (English) - Prairie Provinces.*
2. Canadian poetry (English) - 20th century.*
I. Cooley, Dennis, 1944-

PS8295.5P6I57 1992 C811'.5408'09712 C92-098193-3
PR9198.2.P62I57 1992

this book is for Diane

I would like to thank those who have gone out of their way in making this fragile project happen. Getting the book done has not been easy and it has involved more than a few crises. It owes its existence to the support of the authors themselves, and to their publishers. Without their understanding there would have been no anthology. Most of all it owes its existence to the fervour with which Douglas Reimer pursued writers and publishers in search of permissions. His was a mission, a lover's passion, and I have been blessed to have been found by him. Robert Kroetsch has lent his madly quiet enthusiasm for the anthology from the outset and endured his own share of duty in selecting the poems found on pages 72 to 88. Manuela Dias has prepared the book for the press with a meticulousness that would make a glass cutter feel gauche; Christine Paulos has taken it into the world with her perennial joy; and Pat Sanders—even as I sulked for more space, dallied over my work, pushed deadlines past death, railed for poetry; even as publishers went into clever publisher ploys and poets held off in what little coyness is left to poets—even then Pat Sanders has presided over the whole enterprise with a calm and a resolve that no one in bookdom could ever have shown. *(D.C.)*

Contents

Dennis Cooley

Lorna Crozier

E.F. Dyck

Patrick Friesen

Introduction

Draft, an earlier anthology of prairie poetry which I edited, appeared in 1980. It was meant to be a prospective on new prairie poetry, prospective partly because at the time there was no large body of work and no anthology that sampled widely across the writing. There were several already distinguished poets—John Newlove, Eli Mandel, Robert Kroetsch, to cite the most obvious—but the flood of poetry which since has inundated the dry lands had only begun. And so I selected a few pieces by dozens of writers—61 poets in about 200 pages according to my count—meant to touch the beginnings of the new writing. It was a collection based on currency and promise.

It is now 1992 and this anthology, *Inscriptions*, is meant to be quite another collection. It is not an updated *Draft*, nor is it a sequel to it. *Inscriptions* is retrospective and gathering, meant to bring together those who have long been committed to poetry and to the prairies. It represents more extensively a limited number of poets—18 poets in roughly 300 pages. Every anthologist is bound to fail, can please no one, not even himself. Omissions are painful to authors and readers and editors alike. This is only one anthology; it is not the last word, nor is it even the best word. It is my best word right now. Knowing that, and knowing how differently I myself might have construed this anthology, I want briefly to explain the rationale for including these authors.

One consideration has been residency—imaginative residency. I didn't want to include those who had simply passed through, and I didn't want to feature those who had just arrived, nor did I want to bring in those who physically lived in the prairies but wrote as if they were somewhere else entirely. The writing in some way or other had to show signs that it came out of the prairies or that it engaged with the place. The terms could be loose, then, *were* loose. The place spread into the edges of the Shield and the Rockies, engagements ranged from anecdote to experiment, minute recording to extravagant invention. Poets were as likely to explore structures of knowing as details of landscape, as taken by the play of voicings as quiet meditations. The question of definition, then: who is a prairie poet? who qualifies for consideration?

Another criterion was sustained productivity. I decided early on that I would be looking at those who had published a substantial body of work over a number of years. They would have been committed to the enterprise for the long haul, and they would have a fair track record. As a rule of thumb I told myself that would mean something like four books or so over ten years or more. If the collection were to be retrospective and consolidating and if it were to include those who had participated in the shaping of that conversation it would have to cover that kind of ground.

Quantity, duration, and residency counted for a lot, but no poets were going to get into the collection without signs that their writing was particularly strong or influential. The painful question of value. It should be evident, I hope, that my choices in poets were shaped as much by a larger readership as they were by my own preferences. My championing has entered the list, certainly, but I have felt guided, too, by expectations already formed by others. The criteria for measuring response were broad. Those who had been interviewed, written about, taught, anthologized, nominated for awards, received awards, accorded various forms of respect—those I felt I would be expected to have included—I have largely included. Anthologies are commonly shaped by such conversation—the editor's musings, the editor's sense of what readers might say to him.

I have chosen the individual selections with less sense of obligation. Having for practical reasons decided to consider only poems in books, I read my way through book after book, through every single book published by the authors, as a matter of fact—about 150 as I remember—and, though I have included a few poems mindful of readers' demand, I have selected from them those poems which seem to me most accomplished and most appealing. I especially looked for freshness of language and play with form. I have tried to stress a range in the writing, rejoicing in coming across poems which, even if they were slightly atypical for an author, represented some reach in the writing or some possibility for prairie poetry.

This anthology takes its place alongside another recent anthology from Turnstone—Daniel Lenoski's collection of long prairie poems, *a/long prairie lines*—and, like it, is meant to make readily available a sampling of the skilled poetry coming out of the prairies. I am excited by what is here and I hope readers, too, will be struck with delight as they make their way through the individual poems. I will be pleased if they are as impressed as am I by what these poets have written. *Inscriptions* will, I hope, help us to enter that body of work and to find our way further into the strangely known and wildly unknown terrain that is prairie poetry.

Dennis Cooley

Inscriptions

George Amabile

PRAIRIE

a light word
sun spokes through the overcast
at dusk, or smoke
totems wisping away
into beige emulsions

an earth word
a moist darkness turning
stones and roots
fossils and tiny lives
up to the sky

a watery word
mirage and heat lightning
steadied by pewter barns
where whole towns float in a lilting haze
and rumours of rain rise from the rapeseed lakes

a flame-shaped word
a ragged mane blowing
for miles across dry grass
lighting the night like a battle scene
out of the old testament

a word with air
in its belly that howls
for hours or days and dries
the memory of soft conversation
to wheatdust under the tongue

like the distance we've come
to stand here in the sky at the top of the world

RED RIVER WEDDING

If you stretch out
over the stones, the tree roots
and look down into the shallows
you can see tadpoles and shiny fry
wobble or shoot
through colonnades of reeds
tinted by leaf rot and rock oxides.

Families and friends collect
on the far shore
in the wind, in the meadow grass
where the first blaze changes
driftwood into solid glare
as their voices reach for the old harmonies
and a loose music softens the edge of day.

Children play near the forest
and back out of sight among the trees
the bride remembers trembling
waterlights and leaves
where she sunned herself on the sand
at a bend in the stream
while the groom dreams of horses
and rain.
                    Soon they will step
in their stiff clothes
—ice-frill princess and black knight—
from scrub oak shadow into the light
that turns these tarnished waters into wine.

FIRST KILL

1

I always wanted
to be a great

white hunter.
It wasn't easy

crawling over
the tarpaper roof

of the toolshed
with my *Daisy* carbine

peering down
into the cinders

and grass of the alley
till the big striped

tabby made his move.
Bee bee's rattled

as I lowered my sights.
The smell of machine oil

stoned me. *Pffft.*
Direct hit. But the beast

yowled, spit
back and vamoosed.

2

An accident taught me
how to draw blood.

We were playing
in a lot with broken glass.

Who could throw
the fragments higher.

I winged one out of sight.
It returned, buzzing

and cut the muscle
of Anthony Morga's calf.

3

They're up there
tucked away in struts
and girders of the trestle

cooing and dropping
spatterdung on the street.
I watch them creep

out and rise
with a flurry of wing noise
wheeling in broken arcs

over the city. But
before they leave
their dingy labyrinth

they stop to puff
their chest feathers
and cock their heads.

That's when I'll pull
the inner-tube strips
tight. *Release.* The bottle

chip spins, hissing
cutting his take-off
to a floppy dive. He hits

the sidewalk and sits
there, one wing
flailing the concrete.

I pick him up.
He bleeds into my hands.

4

When the cops pass, I edge
into the alley and run
two blocks to a loose board
in the coal-yard fence.

I can feel his normal fever
against my skin. Why
won't he die? I toss him back
into the air but he can't

fly. When I lift him
again, one eye stares
vacant as garnet. Though his heart
races, he makes no move

to escape. I could leave him
for the cats, or keep him
a secret in my room, but that's
for kids & sisters: this

is where the gang made me
smoke, drink beer, and scratch
its name on my arm; where I jumped
without clothes for a lousy buck

down from the tracks into a hill
of pea coal. No one's here.
I've got that choked feeling
you get the first time

you steal or buy dirty comics.
I've watched my father do it—
loop the string over scaly feet
and hoist them up. Then you squeeze

the beak wide, feed
the blade into his throat
and cut. Shudders. Violent wings.
Blood like royal vomit.

Warm grey feathers come loose
with the sound of ripped stitches.
They're still in the air when I gut him
cut off the head, the feet, then push

a stick through the meat and hold it
over a flaming nest
of brown bags and stained newspaper.

5

Without salt, without water
to wash his death away

the taste was wild, but I chewed
and swallowed even the small wishbone.
I couldn't eat again for days.

MISERICORDIA GENERAL

for Robert Emmet Finnegan

The window
itself can't change
and I can't move
enough to change
what it shows me:
the soiled brick
wall, part of a white
windowframe
four telephone wires:
consciousness distilled
to the space between
this tireless machine that breathes
for me, and a block
of sheltered lives.

The swamp invades
itself   Under scum
and broad pads   green
jaws cruise   Almost
nothing
remembers how
to breathe

Slippery tongs
grip   Suddenly

flesh gives way

A long, slow
slide and I'm
there

My lungs fill and burn

Grand Prairie. I was born
here. Cannonades
of light over the snow
left me
hungry for exotic
wars.
            Hard
to believe, after years
in the signal corps
the great pyramid
cells, the horns
of grey matter, anterior
columns and tracts blown
like power-lines and bridges . . .

Only my eyes move.

At first they brought me
books, turned
pages till I slept.
I blinked messages
like radio code into deep
space. Nothing
got through. I learned
to concentrate on the view.

Today the wall has broken
out in a cold sweat
as though it were ill
as though the whole damn world . . .

But no. By noon
the bricks are dry.
By dusk they're warm and snug.

I'm lying on a bed
of brick that stretches
and curves to the round
horizon   The sky
is a glass kiln   Hot
wind mixed with green
shadow dyes
my hospital gown dark
as a forest   The bricks
glow   Thick
smoke all around
me then the gown bursts
into flame   Ashes
float   I can't
feel a thing but waves
that melt in the air make
my eyes water   and open
to darkness that thins
as the wall returns . . .

Of course it's not just
a wall; it's earth, pulverized
rock, shaped
by fire and sweat—lore
old as the Chaldees.

I remember
the mason I worked for once
(the exact mouth, face
baked like a mask of the desert
under a shock of white
hair, the spare
frame, crooked fingers
eyes bright as a hawk's)

digging his loam in October
letting it powder under the frost
mixing the weathered remains with spring

water, ground chalk, ashes
bone meal, coal dust or dried
seeds pounded to grist, tempering this
to a smooth pug with his feet
culling and kneading each clot
lifting it over his head
slamming it down into the slick
or sanded beechwood mould and stockboard
squaring the top with a wet strike

lugging the raw brick on pallets
up to the drying ground
laying them in a scintle hack
under straw to cure in the air

stacking up codes in a kiln
he knew he'd have to break
and build and break and build
again, every three years

kindling the fire holes
with twigs and paper
"to drive off water smoke"
raising the heat with stove logs
then charcoal.
                              Seal the arches
let it cook for a week.

I'd help him draw the cooled stock
astonished at the way some change
in temper, heat or stack pattern
could produce shades
of red from scarlet to blood
pudding, pinks, browns, ocher, sulphur
buff   orange and grey
to green or woodsmoke blue.

And they weren't just bricks, but phrases
of a composition he kept
in his head, some chimney, garden walk
or fireplace or gateway
and maybe, if the client could pay
a glazed puzzle that would resolve
into emblems, a coat
of arms, a dignified profile, scenes
from daily life.
                    He worked
all over the world, and worked on the day
he died at ninety-four: single
withe, cavity walls, header
and stretcher, spreading the beds
furrowing and parging, buttering ends
keeping the plumb line straight
to the rim of the course
raking or beading or tuck pointing.

English bond, Flemish bond
running bond and cross bond
garden wall and herringbone and Sussex
noggings and surrounds
pillars, arches and quoins
(I studied this, there
in the war) strapwork
guagework, dentil sets
and rusticated patterns.

Out in the high sun
finishing a patio or pool, tap tap
tap, and the brick, fieldstone
flagstone, tile, would crack
a perfect closer.

    Night   The siren
    gives up its pewter
    ghost   Time

is a glass shock
wave that evaporates
nerve ends *The first*
mortar explodes
the dark like a brimstone
flower I'm over
the hill at last but the same
habits cry
the dragon back
from her peace Reeds
now, hollow
music. Whatever
it touches bleeds. "I'm flying
without support ahead
of the storm There are no
thresholds Everything
is now"
This
is what we were
taught to fear, this play
of self in the snow
taste of remembered
mornings, in the long
dark, empty of almost
anyone else, but it
sings this way
of touching the near
silence where all
the mind can reach
and become and allow
to fade fills
even a desolate
street with spring
light that slowly
explodes my cropped
view of the world

From the top right hand
corner, telephone lines
like an empty musical
staff, drape down
and away

electron streams
vowels and voice
colours blurred
to a hum

where birds come
to rest. Somewhere
they have nests and futures.

This time
it's a grackle, ugly
eyes, feathers glistening
like Texas crude, the beak
opens and I hear, inside,
the sound of a stone
breaking, like the cracked note
of the bugle that played taps
at Arlington for J.F.K.

Life has these necessary
flaws that say don't
gloat, each triumph
is shadowed by invisible failures
all of them real, though disguised
by ritual observance.

Sunfoil flashes
Aerosol   Aerosol   Aerosol

Backpacks and party girls
Police out on the roads

Courage, old heart
somewhere in this
paradigm, the lion sleeps.

I had lost count
of the days, the nights, jars
of glucose hung like sterilized
fruit. Could I have
known how immeasurable
sleep would be
redeemed by bricks? Like faces
in a stadium, they look
the same but have their own
wrinkles and weather
marks, perhaps
the white
of efflorescence, chipped
or blackened by years
of soot to formal death
letters—diverse
histories, none of them
perfectly true.

Cockle shells
Cockle shells

To warm the heart?
No. The sea
is cold. Deep
fissures in a
thunderhead. I should
have been that.

Sometimes (in dreams?
I don't always recognize
that shift out of every day) bricks
burn and pulse like blood
cells, their ember

fire darkening
at dusk when some
of the windowframe ignites
and glows, yellow
through soft curtains.
I have imagined a woman
in that room, singing
her name to myself
watching her intelligent eyes
in conversation. Soon, we will touch.
Our skins will heat and cool in the dark.
There will be children
and friends whose lives
bind ours to the world.

(I know that's not true
or perfect. I know the film
that keeps insight
from outlook, but why
should I care? Death
itself can only hurt
as much as a drawn
shade. I've got
what many say
they want:
no worries, no pain
no one to fight with
no one to blame

and nothing left
to account for.)

Though I can't see
the sun, I can watch
its moods, modes
and seasons, the day
changing—fierce or soft
with mist—rain, leaves

loose in the wind, shadows
of smoke opening, the shadow
of a gull's keen glide
the snow arriving, straight
or swirled, ice
that shines and runs.

A white horse gallops
across the field
into a still
cloud, and the west
blue rings like an anvil.

Here, there is time
to dream a new life
before death, before
the 'copters bursting in air
the sudden drill
of pain in my head
the mud, the lasting silence.

BASILICO

1

Three plants
in one styrofoam cup.
A gift from a friend.

Their smell dissolves
the afternoon, brings back
my grandfather's garden, Sunday

and *pomidoro* sauce in a cast iron pot,
guests arriving in old cars from the city
soft nights, mandolins and laughter

under the window where I fought
off sleep, only to ride
my mother's clear soprano into dreams.

2

Something's wrong. Flooded
with sun on the windowsill, their leaves
go brown at the edges.

I drench them with mist
and sing to them in southern Italian
but it does no good. They suffer

as we do from too much
togetherness. I pull away
the puffed-rice cup, crumble

the earth ball and tug their nest
of roots apart. It sounds
like thin stitches ripping.

3

In their new pots, they have the look
of radical exiles, resentful
and sullen. I put them out

in the spring sun to heal. All evening
at the concert hall, *Le Ballet Jazz*
erases their claim on my heart

until I wake in the dark and feel them
wilting under a late frost.
I go out on bare feet and retrieve them.

4

All day I set them in different windows
following the sun, watching
the light arrange new moods

for the house. When evening comes
I spray their limp
dishevelled leaves and give them

up to the dark.
Awake
with the first light, I'm surprised
and happy to see their pumped up leaves

drinking the dawn. I decide
to celebrate, pour a cold beer
into the tall green glass

I found in my mother's cupboard
after she died. I hold it up
to the window, watch

the bubbles rise and bolt
it back. A warm jolt spreads
from my stomach up to my brain

and it's only then that I notice
how their stems lean
over, trying to sleep. So I push

a pair of stained chopsticks
into the soil and tie their heads
up straight. But when I pull

back to admire my artfulness, the edge
of my hand brushes the glass
and it falls to the floor. The sound

it makes as it shatters trips
the same stab of panic I had
to control as a child whenever she left

the room. I see her perched on a stool
at the stove in her small house, drained
by cancer, cooking the last

meals of her life. I bend
and sweep up the curved shards, green
as my birthstone, brokenly

musical as they slide
from the dustpan into the trash.
The room fills with more and more light.

And it all comes close again: Her wisdom.
Her temper. Her cuisine. No one
has ever got her tomato sauce right

though she gave us her secret freely:
Five or more leaves of fresh basil.
Half an afternoon at moderate heat.

douglas barbour

SUMMER'S SEA SON:

schtosh   schtoosh   osh   osh
schtoshtosh   tish

sch schtun

osh shun   osh shun
osh shun   osh sun
o sun   o sun   o sun   o sun ash tone

ash ton ish   meant
ash schton ish sh
ash   stone   ash stone ash   stun

ashshallow   ash shallow   shallow   swallow

ash sh   schton   ish   ish   ish   shallow

shal low   shal low   shal low

shal om   shal lom   sh sh shal lom

shallow   shal low   shal om   shalom   osh

shun   osh shun   osh shun   oshun

OUR LADY OF THE SLOWLY FREEZING LAKESHORE — NOVEMBER:

icy icy icy icy i see i sing i see i sing i sing
ice see ice see ice sea ice see ice sing ice sea
ice shift ice shift ice shift ice d r i f t iceshift ice d r i f t

ice sail ice sail cul ice sail cul icesailcul ice sail kill
icicle icicle icicleicicleicicle i sailkillice sail kill icicle icicle ice
sail cul icicle ice sail kill icicle i see kill sail ice sail cul
i see cold icicle i see cold Icicle i see cold icicle i see
icy icy icy icy i c y i see ising icing cold ice sail
cool ice sail cool i sing cold ice sail cool i sing cold ice
seal kill ice seal kill icesealkill ice sail cul icesealkill
ice cycle ice cycle slicecycle ice cycle slicecycle ice
cycle ice is ice is ice is ice is ice

is ice is ice is ice isice isice isice is ice
is ice is ice is ice is ice is ice is ice is
Isis is Isis is Isis shift ice is is Isis is

ice is is ice is is Isis

is ice sail cool i sing

Isis

is ice is is ice is

is ice

SONG 19:
and the rain it raineth every day

rain song   variations on
a theme of
roofs leaves sidewalks
grass:
            the hiss of
tires   and wires
singing in
   the whipping wind

   or   steady thrum on
         wood and glass
   the thrash of
         sudden heavy storm:
               thunder as a
         background chorus

         rim shots of hail   exploding
   everywhere   upon
         occasion

   we sit cool in
   side   and watch
   the long slanting fibres   hair
   awash in air   strand by
         strand   entwine
            our grey grey
   days
         we listen
   to the shifting
         endless
            song:

SONG 61:

What does poetry do
then? he asked me
not having liked my poems,
not thinking them 'poems' at all he said .

& what could i say to him i had
nothing to offer beyond
(the poems) /

& i have
no answer for you
no answer that would do
what you want it to, what
you want me to
do, writing poems
for you / for

what? that you might say
you liked them / & who
else .

All else failing this answer:

If possible, poetry sings .
Sings poetry, if possible .

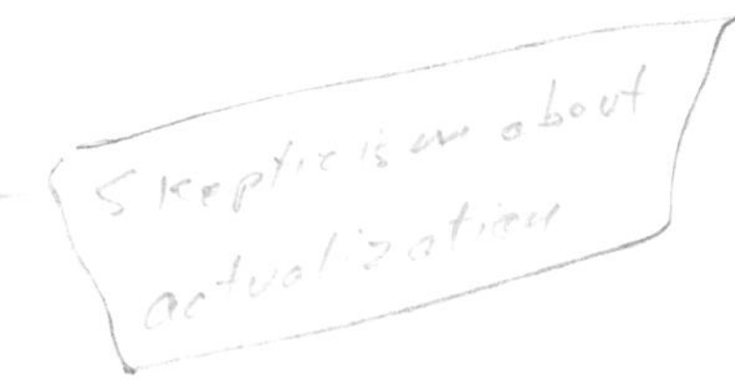

no answer / no response
in his eyes / i
could not be seen could not be
heard?

i must still
however
sing .

SONG 64:
new year's eve—new year's morning / 71-72:

Listen!   it is cold /
                    the air
is clear   the sky is clear
    tonight   the stars are all there
turning with us here
    below their   clearlight

out .   out there
    they sing / the planets sing

                    still, whether

you believe it or not / I am listening

are you there?   who
    cares?   where
        are you
              anyway?

the stars sing   the planets
            sing
in their blue orbits
    & tonight it is cold & we might hold
each other extra tight
    for warmth

while we listen
    to their song
              & just perhaps

for warmth

we'll sing along .

SONG 65:
blues in january / 1:

i said:
how often have i seen
this scene / with cold eyes
coldly taking in its frigid beauty:
white   just white
everywhere,   the groping
trees   the sky   the land
hidden beneath this cold blank stare
of the weather

i said: i have seen this
before,   & admired it .

It is so pure
& so cold   i dont
know how to see it again

again & again i see
things i think i know

i dont know / what i have seen
i said:

SONG 89:
the cross / country railway song:

the railrhythm railrhythm
speaks it is a
continuous word
the syllables
run with the wheels   (lots of consonants &)
a steady rhythm   yes

it says so much for just one word
unheard & heard   an earth
ly beauty trees sing
                                        such long words
each time / across a country
that is the word we listen for

carved like a rune
on the block of a world displayed
to time's bleak gaze

parts of the carved word are chipped or worn,
a word in ruins nearly
but still there / still heard

each time the train moves   speaking
one long word
no longer heard clearly
no longer listened for by more
than a few staring listeners, slow
of hearing,   slow
of passage,   listening
across vast space to
the word / unheard .

BREATH GHAZAL NUMBER 11

ok spring   ive got you figured   this time
returning   breath for breath   filling

you inhale   slow inebriation   you
breathe out the growth,   widening green

every shade of   intoxication   non toxic
photosynthesis   filling the trees & grass

buds swell   they fill with fresh air
inhaled   sunlight   &   they   are   a light

for a few days only   you can almost hear them
brightly breathing in the sharp spring air

STORY FOR A SASKATCHEWAN NIGHT

for Robert Kroetsch

> Picnic in a coulee in a cow pasture. . . .
> But I couldn't tell a story. The
> novelist unable to tell a story.
> The ghost of my father, there in the
> shadows—the story-teller.
>
> *The 'Crow' Journals*
> (Friday July 25 1975
> Qu'Appelle Valley)

i

coyotes maybe hidden nearby   i
am silent   the ghost in
the shadows waiting to speak   but
i am silent   listen

no   there is
no story   that
is what i have to tell you

i have to tell you   there
is no story tonight   there
is no story here   listen
there are all too many stories
clamouring   &
i have to tell you   i
cant tell them

if the cowshit could speak   it would tell you
nothing   no   well
nothing you dont already know
& the grass
talks on   of dying   of dying
to feed the goddamned cows

(this isnt narrative   hell
its not even complaint

the flames die too
& their story wont stay still
you cant follow
the changes   modulations

the sky
is full of stories   those bright
eyes looking down
on the prairie   i
cant begin to tell you   about

listen   all
the stories you wont hear
about that train now
its long roar fading
in the dark

no   now that we know
theres no story at all
we can begin to tell it

listen

ii

what the silence said
was nothing   nothing
we could listen to

we could *hear*

the silence   it
wasnt saying anything
but stories   stars spatter
                  on the night sky

that train   dopplers away
whooeee   WHOOOEEEEE
we hear that tale
everyday   each night
of its retreat   running
a storyteller   not
saying a word
into the dark   &   away
from some
                  place

or the cows
no longer seen   but
listen   their stories
are   shumpff   mumchpht   chumpff
the chewing over of what vast
metaphysics   the grass
also refuses   to speak
or the crickets

the writer refused
        to tell a story
or   no   the writer
told us   he
        couldnt tell us
a thing   &

we listened   again
to the silence   no
silence   &

all it had
            to say

iii

or some other
possibility:

the yawning air
says   open
wide   theres a sky   now
swallow it all
                  empyrean

there   curved high above us
as the darkness deepens

more stories   appear
                              silent
insistent
            listen

            & sky
            tells another blue story
            of fucking sweet earth
            down there   way off   where
            they meet
            in utter silence as usual
                                    (can you
                  see it   where
                  one darkness   solid
                  touches another   clear

            at the end of the road
                  end of the valley
                  end of the lake
                  end of the
                              world

or the story
so far away
& not telling it again
of course

iv

the sky opening
the land the land the sky

they keep repeating they
keep repeating they
have nothing to say &
they say that they
say we say
theres nothing here
can you hear it

each time they
repeat it each time
i believe it i believe
theres nothing more to say

theres more nothing to say

theres more

or driving
the point home driving
again along the prairie
seeing what has not been said

& saying it
s saying it

that theres nothing to say
& *that* grows

i said
listen/
or look

its all around you
all those stories   you
want told
or it does

listen
: one moon   only
a howling below

all that   empty   filling
with the stories we dont believe
we can tell

& we re telling them

v

plenitude   O
prairie   /   plenitude

it unfolds
nothing

is what it says

the sky   e g   un
folding   blue
no
thing   crisscrossed
labyrinths of cloud
unspeaking   un
speakable   grey   rain

there is no room for
a short space   a
short poem here   you
must expand   to fill
the space with words

stories   youll
never tell   yes

but who wouldnt ‘sing’
either   saying only

the lines of
type perhaps
that rush against the window

nothing to say
the rain says
dont listen

the prairie unfolds
so much expressive shading
tones say in
spring fall
a loss or abundant
shifts of (tones) mud
soaked in rain
fall saying
nothing

it didnt hurt
you dont have to say
anything you
mustnt cry

it unfolds then
now unfolds mystery

& that is what it wont tell
& that is what it cant tell
& that is what it
tells you

i have
nothing
to say

ssshhhshshshshsh shsh sh sh

a few colours hey
is it spring or
fall which
few colours what
signs

that hasnt been said
or you weren't listening
or it *wasnt* a story

that time

say will be held against you
all that pain
you cry why
me so far from
comforting sky or
grassy hills or
not
that horizon
split with light
a way off

silence

an abundance of
absence
you know

you forget
the catalogue
of desire

it grows

the seeds
grow it
opens
wider
it refuses

to speak

vi

this is not
absence simply

the presence
of absence

theres a story here
not to be told

unspeakable
i cant
tell it

nothing to say
nothing to say
nothing to say
nothing to say
nothing to say

of black earth
of the crops tall
wind-swept waves
of wheat say the
harvest coming

in silence

say silence

again

TWO WORDS / TOWARDS

To ward
off what
event   you
allow to
die into
any known
now .   Now
you say
it   now
you dont .
Night falls
in unrest
but all
the rest
is this
unknown silence
'you' call
thru to
'me' .   Why
do I
allow it .
I never
can say
goodbye   nor
why I
came to
you this
unknown way /
unknowing pray
for some
new now
lost sound
of reflection
reflecting off
the water

to say
'I' or
'you' . You
can only
say 'I
know what
you feel'
once . Twice
now you
had me
at your
mercy, twice
you let
me go .
Now 'I'
would stay .
I would
say Let
night fall
since all
you do
is go
away . I
am lost
again: 'in
love' I
might say
but you
wont believe
that . We
hear as
thru a
glas darkly
doubled . Why
should 'you'
care what
'I' say .

I say
what I
believe my
heart knows .
But who
knows anyones
heart now .
Now I
will say
it: 'I
love you .'
But who
speaks now
who spoke
before 'I'
said it .
I dread
it   seeing
I will
say and
never know
for sure
all that
I say .
And none
can say
precisely what
is meant
by that .
A retreat
to origins
of feelings
known only
in saying
and always
said always
before 'I'

or 'you'
say them .
This is
going nowhere .
Where can
'I' find
the first
beginning beginning
what I
have to
say now .
I dont
know . Know
only that
such knowledge
is already
spoken / written
down for
'me' to
ask it
questions . Where
am I
going then .
Towards two
words that
must meet
in us:
this I
not 'I'
this you
not 'you'
will complete
some looked
for conjunction
only connecting
two words
to ward

off what .
Event .   'You'
allow it .
Lie down .
What is
said here
is hear
say .   Saying
again what
has always
already been
said .   We
are together
here gathered
to be
those two:
just 'I'
just 'you' .

E.D. Blodgett

WEASEL

before you grass
the green had never heard

before you no
silence no mouth sowing
green under wind

before then, before an o
you merely began
and your eyes i might have said
were stones and mute

if the air seemed dark
the stone sunned

only the wind moved
winding where your ear
entranced as a first alpha
reared against your head

the wind only moved
and in some ancient tongue he spoke

and when he spoke, you said
myself:
                the grass you heard reply

and yourself you heard
through airs of the green wind
decline across the ground

o early alpha
o mary mary what seed then
came so holy down within your ear
and said myself again
where the god sole sprang

and stone flamed and grass
grown within your mouth

and into your tongue the small beasts
unwind, your mouth brooding,
where the world all enclosed
utters word

when autumn comes again
and cold, and blue jays, streaked
incisions in the air, descend,
the air shrieks, as if

but field and tree were ripped
and flesh.
                    as if air, opened,
speaks.

ELEPHANTS

what could they mean, the early nights so thick
with stars and the moons turning where they dream,
light falling on their round and paleolithic
sleep? what would redeem

them, their breath running tidal up the great
shores of air where through them all earth
would breathe and rivers for the winds create?
theirs is the first birth

of birds, and the long crimson song of birds,
and others calling 'yellow' where yellows appear
flowered in air as fragrant echoes of words.
so in dream they hear

where they go when they die: some to where the green
would burst, and others after blue. their death
but flowers returned across the earth is seen,
and bees within their breath

are drawn, some diving into seas of red,
bees chanting *'deo jubilate'*
where drops of yellow into air are shed
and golden is the day.

there is the earth unrolled again in air,
bees garnering praise, where earth sings
earth, and earth through flowers ever repair-
ing to herself and sacred springs.

URSA MAJOR

borne almost over wave, and bent
for colchis once, the ships and then
as forests against a shore the high sea
flowered, and toward the sun the flowers
coursed, where the sea within the furrows sang,
and sailors, and flowers golden and open
flowed wine.

after colchis, and after ulysses ran
behind the sun, the last ships hove
where barely over wave the sole star
hangs.
            o thin in the white nights
voices staring north of the sailors wane
we heard, and stars revolve, the greater bear

dive under wave and rise again,
the choraled cold coming down.
                                        alone
the bear they seek, mounting over black,
and the sea flushed pale against the sky.

to wait she turns there strewn with spray
where flowers fall, bearing ever north,
and where the huge wrecks hive, she falls,
as the hymning sailors slide.
                                   o night, white
roses she bears them round the star, and bees
over wave their boreal tribute pour.

FOR DUCKS
Provincial Museum, Edmonton

1

certain ends cannot be known, but to be
cortés, to seize aztecs in a glass net,
to say, 'now it will snow,' and watch the snow
start and fall and stop—who would not want
to sit with cortés, after all the blood was washed
up, staring at the snow falling over mexico

all white? as if every road i ever walked
took me here, to see the prairie grass as it might
have been, all roads ending in museums where light
like the snow of hernán cortés falls across at will
the thin sloughs and painted floors of grass
where antelope may have run, memories of ducks,

and snakes wrapped in their dreams of rabbits,
burrows cut away and pressed against the glass.
i wanted to weep, and what tears that fell
formed translucent pearls on my cheeks. perhaps
cortés returned to spain encased in glass
drops, and no one saw, for he shone like a god come back.

2

such long afternoons you would say i'd become
walt whitman under glass, loafing and loving, gazing
at the gentle bodies of men and women and children
who gaze at me as one staring into void,
strolling through nathan phillips square before
they are all gone into dark, all

forgotten, brooding through the endless summer
afternoons. 'whose generation is mine?' i wanted
to ask, 'and what should i recall?' somewhere
i wanted to walk where the wind leaves the grass
unmoved, and perhaps then i shall see my friend
of so many other decades ago.

> (o, let me be sly
> when he goes by:
> i shall rise and bow
> the way they showed us how
> when he and i were boys,
> and we would make no noise,
> and none should see
> but he and me)

but where do they go when the light is gone?
is it i alone here, here where the small
windows are closing over canada, waiting
for them all to return, passing hand in hand?
perhaps i should sit with eagles, the glass marbles
beneath their brows chilling in the dark. here

valleys are quick to reach: a step down
and you touch the wall of other mountains, other
streams where under the shaded lights of day
they fall losing themselves. say, will they see
me here, beside the sweet and silver stream,
gazing at silence and the perfect world?

3

better to say: 'walt whitman it is
not, nor ever could have been.' these
windows are time foreclosed, and after them
all appears as negative—the washed air, the shades
of other antelopes surfaced across a slough,
slow mirages exposing.

how many ducks among the reeds, cold and bloodless,
heads gone forever, and only their split tails
placed broken on the floor of water, how many ducks,
and what mouth wailing *quaaa*, stopped in midstream,
its time removed? such ducks as i had seen moving
through small waters near batoche, batoche

where holes spattered on the rector's wall open
to the white sun as light passing through film
falls against a screen. how have i entered this
bloodless space, where are the rifles and faces
shot away, retreats and other rites? what time
do these other ducks move through, echoing

up the saskatchewan, all noise theirs?
how near they come to move as angels move,
simulacra of ducks to say what ducks would be
if there were ducks to see. o, as they pass,
ask them: 'where are the roads that lead to batoche,
what roads to canada, where are the forts, the glass

wall around the plains of abraham, and what has not
cried *quaaa* turning to glass?' batoche beyond
the ends of roads has gone, so platonic
now in the endless beginning, not to be seen
but as shades cast in the endless light
of saskatchewan, beyond ducks and into panes of air.

4

nothing now to do but lie down with ducks,
ducks without name, ducks in the little sloughs,
and ask: 'do ducks get lost?' and hear them feed
serenely in the grass—to know whether birds
playing and feeding in the gentle reeds, should ever
see themselves as ducks flattened on the water's face.

EPISTRE DÉDICATOIRE
(prologue)

How many summers of the Iroquois
they stood, perfectly anonymous,
merely green, and nothing in their dreams
of Adam's late coming, slipping between
them, Adam, inexorable sailor sailing up
the blue and vaginal expanse, his mouth

a lexicon, his eye the eye of God.
For some, to be born is enough, to know the summer
sun in the green heat, the nameless beasts
running to no end in the infinite shade,
a music in the air without words,
knowing the fall of snow, unacclaimed,

unowned, only to fall, the kingdoms where
it falls but words, and everyone alert,
entering fables, their dreams monstered: o
to be reborn, all the stories new,
to run through far kingdoms, eyes charged
with myth, into invisible snow, the mists,

the virgin trees, instruments in hand!
Fable, astrolabe, and genesis
at last, one book and one law,
the trees of Hochelaga and Adam's eye
all one, the fables carried home,
everything exposed, the rest unsaid.

LEAVING LOUISBOURG (N.S.)

Nothing lives here: even the birds
are cut from the sky—small kites, they hang
above a paper sea, their thin dreams
eyeing fish within the paper depths.
I fear the touch of stone, and fear the sea
where ships stand pressed against the sky,
ships I cannot walk around, ships

at bay where the birds scream, gazing down,
as I would want to scream, flat sounds
unrolling from my mouth, the words spelt
to echo something said in French, words
recalled, uttered outside, places where
grass grows from green to brown, and ships
lean under wind: o, the water,

what were the words for water? To call it forth,
to put it on, screens of pale green,
to see fish wakes streaming down your arms,
to dance wet in the streets, past fronts
of shops, the tower where the clock keeps pace
with times across the sea, to say: "Praise!
Praise the earth, the long arrival of green

realities of birds, the turning in arcs,
soundless curves in the opening air, the mute
reply of praise, its semaphore and shade—
praise in the walk of horses, praise in the trace
of rain falling, the deep praise of fish,
cosmos of roots praising earth, light
bending in space (quick dance of grass,

the dance of air)!" To hear figures arrive
applauding, the sound coming from their hands
of clapping written on the air, and up
beyond our small stage of France it goes
saying *louange* against the sky. I see
we are here forever, all speaking hung
within the air, cast off, nowhere to go

above the fort, the brief paper street.
I fear to say *farewell*, pretend we walk
the earth, to see whatever I say become
bird, blank sign in the dome of space,
absence shaped. I see there is no out
from here, but only in, reaching the sill
of speech—the awkward trees we see and ships

calling connotations in the air.
But what do they mean, the deathless ships, the trees
against the shore? How shall I speak them, their bare
shape, untouched, almost the sky? Do they wait?
Has something gone? How shall I say *They came?*
How utter France, how shall I start,
strung from word to word, to read back

from this sky, beyond the void where birds
are drawn, and images of houses where
the air is squared in glass? Teach me to breathe,
to open the fence of speech, to see ships
rise against the sky and birds return,
the emptiness of space closed: to breathe,
to move seamless into fire, forget

this bay of false starts, of grave suspense
where water at your feet falls dead,
where every rock, the coast and strange birds,
this house of marionettes, edge the sky
with proverbs. Teach me the things of speech, to speak
praise and hear flowers burst from my mouth,
lions leaving the air flagged in shreds.

MÉTIS

Speak the great names: Fort Qu'Appelle,
St Isidore de Bellevue, Grand Coteau,
Batoche, Fort Walsh, Frog Lake and Cut Knife Hill,
Seven Oaks and the rest of Rupert's Land,
and say what lies there between: bones
the wind gives back, bones of buffalo, bones
of the hunters, bones of Blackfoot, Cree and Blood,
the prairie piled white with hunts, all
bone brothers under sun. Name
me, Gabriel, king of this bare kingdom

of bones, riding and riding through white remains.
Name me, Gabriel, hero of the Wild
West of Buffalo Bill, hero of the great
Staten Island shoot out, me and Le
Petit, killers of little blue balls,
riding and riding through pictures of sage brush and sky,
fighting with clocks beneath the electric sun,
never as we used to fight, waiting,
talking, never arriving though miles and miles
of coulee and plain. And now where the prairie was

Sitting Bull and I and faces in the dark
square off, Chief of the great Hunkpapa Lakota,
dazed in the painted flats, and I, calling,
calling: God, will they find us, lost in faces,
before we stop forever, smiling in a glass
cage, where rivers stop, and birds hang
on the sky never moving? My smile is glass.
Everything lies inside me: buffalo run
to ground, streets I never saw where the elms
line faces singing white, singing

"The Stars and Stripes Forever," waiting for wars
and other shows at the town's end. They see
me, Gabriel, and see a war that hardly
was, a circus war so put off we almost
missed the last call. Dummies I gave
them to save my friends, men stuffed like the great
chief and I who drift slowly through places
and then through names where hundreds walk to gaze
and conjure us. Speak the names—me, Gabriel,
a clock ticking to an abandoned house.

EXPLORER

Gone. Not one that asked which way was north.
What does it mean the south inverted so?
And some never spoke, gathering notes
in little books, rushing up the rivers,
away, their eyes open everywhere,
huge as lakes, no thing, no

hill, no emptiness beyond
that was not there reflected—flat, reversed
and floating past: so are Kelsey's eyes,
rhyming *fate* with *late*, to see his shade
always farther ahead and entering trees
days before he enters his notes, to see

fate, arrive and find it gone, always
too late, sight rhymes for a fiction un-
seen. Or other eyes, La Vérendrye's,
seizing the syllables of trees in French
where they speak, edging the wide shores with green
words, outlines falling apart at summer's end.

They are all—MacKenzie, Henry, Jacques Cartier—
maps of eyes, how many miles of degrees
falling cleanly through them, outsides marked
and put away, lakes whose surface lies
soundless, other, and all that's mirrored there
is wet—trees, canoes, hills and sky—

dripping from fingers moving away from south,
latitudes drowning wherever you take the world
in. Why do you ever come back, your backs turned,
gazing dully through strata and degrees,
to tell us, as Rupert Brooke would one day say:
"A godless place. And the dead do not return"?

How shall we sing the godless, the not yet
dead? O name the long measure of the world
where outlines lie before us on a page,
black notes against the white surveyed—
as one might turn north to music scored
for flutes, to rhyme *death* with *breath*, the air

figuring itself, proleptic and sure,
going always into itself, without
edges, no shade but lengths of light
refracted and still. Other music, the trees
transmuted to a speech of gods we cannot hear,
unwritten, grace notes without design.

PAVANES

1

I cannot find the note: it was a sound
that calls and calls. It comes, perhaps, from green—

the green of rainy birds who leave the air
green when they are gone. Or is it now

someone says: 'Yesterday I heard
it in the air, a note that fell across

my skin as rain, bare music that when
it falls it disappears within the ground,

the rain gone.' I cannot recall who spoke
so of rain, who told me of the grass

greener after rain, and yet I want to touch
nothing but green, music and air becoming

2

green, unable to see
the space before my eyes
but mere humility
of nightingales and signs,

gardens, gardens and
the way that damsels walk
in innocence, their hand
untouched. To hear them talk

was such to make the air
a green thing before
my eyes, nothing there
but echo, nothing more

and tales of sudden death,
wings in the air, an end
of sense, becoming breath:
can innocence pretend,

gardens, music, rain
idyllic alone within
the eye, the rest insane—
not seen, not green, akin

to tales of nightingales,
no song but words distilled
in blood? Nothing avails
when music lies killed

3

and nightingales a residue of words.
is this the song she sang, the voice that came
upon me once in Spain beside the sea,
a voice with evening flowers taking root
within her mouth, and through the flowers bright
and golden bees, sipping as she sang,

and birds in twilight calling from the shade
in unknown tongues, remembering the rain,
the warped trees across the plain, the grass
and flowers near the sea? But this was not
the song she sang, dwelling within her dark
throat, her voice that took the cloth of air

and left it on the ground, an old thing
for other birds to bear away, a song
of autumn tragedies, the sudden wreck
of green and gardens near the sea, her song
that entered flowers, spoke of blood, and where
the nightingale had sung, she sang of change,

o alchemies of throats, the bloodied air,
and old morphologies within the dark
of swallow, nightingale and other birds
that streak the air with songs that never end,
speaking of final things ever *da capo,*
flowers alive, bees within their throats

4

and one lament
within the Orphic air: I see
the song, and she
is flower, the air

breaking where her mouth
receives
the song and brevities
of bee,

red fountains
spilling through the air,
bare
space of season,

eternal play
of summer,
and no flower
the same

again.
Flowers are a rhyme
that nullify time
turning

on themselves,
flowers singing of rain
and pain
and accidents of nightingales,

a voice
that speaks of eschatology,
how I, perhaps, am she,
a nightingale or

5

music that flowers
under rain and golden bees,
no refrain to hear

6

but flowers opening beside the girl.
Is this where season is, nothing but what

it is: flower, fountain, damsel or
the moment when the riders entered, the space

of flowers opening and three riders
coming to drink and gaze upon the ground?

it does not say how long they gazed, nor how
they spoke, nor when they parted how their fingers

grazed, but into summer the riders rode,
past the bee and nightingale, and one

by one they fell beside the road, the rain
upon their shirts, the flowers bleeding, the sea

without sound. Or is it when the horses
passed, their saddles empty? 'No flower, no

bee can touch me where I am,' she said.
'I am not season, nightingale or rain,

7

nor shall I speak of rings I gave,
nor why their eyes were hard and black,
nor when I spoke to them of love
they bent their heads and looked

away, speaking of fate alone
and how they could not stop until
their foes were met and laid upon
the ground. They would not tell

the rest, but drank from wooden cups
the water I gave, and when our fingers
met, I saw how each did weep
then turn away, the tears

spilling slowly down to earth.
Nor would my brothers tell me more
but words within the rain of death:
I saw it was the air

that wept, not they, the emptiness
of gardens in my eyes, the sign
of nightingales that spills across
my face, and from the sea

8

barest whispers on the sand.' And so
she sang, nothing in the air to see
but measured sounds of her mortality,

dying beneath the fall of rain, nothing
she is but the pitch of green becoming green,
not bees but murmurings of bees within

the throats of flowers, not flowers but
silence steeping the air, and where they rode,
the sound of horses on the plain, no sun

but suns that she would sing, nor moon to mark
the night, the air of all breathing things,
the sea become music in her mouth.

Elizabeth Brewster

ON THE DEATH BY BURNING OF KIMBERLY HAMMER, MAY 1972

Only the grandmother weeps—
the mother smiles, tearless,
the father also,
though panic clouds his eyes,
an effort
not to see.

A neighbour remembers
the child Kimberly
out walking at Christmas
wrapped for winter,
cheeks pink, eyes bright as candles,
saying,
"I like to walk in the cold. I like the cold."

When fire blazed through the tent,
when there was no cold,
did your young eyes see
all past and future blazing at once?

Knowing you will miss
our gradual years
the slow burn
of time in your flesh,
we are not sure
if what we feel is pity
or is envy.

Later, at night,
I awake cold in bed,
pile on winter blankets,
make a tent
of skin and blankets.

I sleep again, and dream
of you, Kimberly,
no child of mine, no relative,
a May candle
burning
in the dark.

SUMMERS HERE AND THERE

June is cold this year.
Rain and wind bend the green billowing trees.
A lawn chair left on the balcony
would likely blow away.

And I am homesick for somewhere
where it's really summer,
for blowsy heatwave days
with drooping peonies on humid lawns

and willows trailing
their green sweating hair
in river water

or even for streets
where men with carts
sell ice-cream cones
at corners
and someone plunks a tune
on a guitar
and artists draw
for a few coins
with chalk on sidewalk.

I remember somewhere
some time
hot fragrant nights
the hot chirr
of a crickety insect sound
and the damp smell of earth
steaming up to my window.

And now that time is here for me.
I have created it
out of the smell of rain
and the slithering sound
of the cars sliding past
on the wet street

dark coming on
this cold June
I come back to.

MAP OF THE CITY

"Beautiful Saskatoon,
potash capital of the world,"

the map is labelled.

No population figures given
but 135,000 in January 1975
so they say at the Public Library.

On the front of the map, in colour,
Saskatoon on a late June day.
View across the bridge from the south side of the river
to the Bessborough Hotel,
a fortress Gothic
as the early twentieth century
could build,

guarding the city hall
some shops and churches;
beyond, green fields,
and above, the sky as blue and infinite
as when I look out at it now
from my window
(after that thunderstorm in the night).

See, when you open the map
it is divided
almost exactly in two
by the slant of
the South Saskatchewan River
running from corner to corner.

From my side (north)
and the shops, police station, post office
I cross daily
over one of these bridges.
The map does not show
the cars, trucks, bicycles, buses
and how they creep at rush hour
and it does not show the bridge on a windy day
or the fine dust blowing
into the mouths of pedestrians.

On the north side
the streets are mostly numbered
(except for Saskatchewan Crescent
by the river
and some on the far outskirts)
but on the south side
there are also streets with names:
University Drive and College,
and Temperance to remind us
that Saskatoon was founded
by Methodist Total Abstainers
from Ontario;

Colony and Garrison
(how Canadian);

and to the far south
a group of streets named for girls and trees:
Isabella, Adelaide, Ruth,
Maple, Willow, Elm, Ash.

Almost off the map,
on the right,
are streets named
Harvard, Cambridge, Yale,
McGill, Carleton,
Dalhousie, Mount Allison,
Waterloo, McMaster,
Simon Fraser.

The map shows
parks, open spaces, transit systems, schools,
It lists
recreation units, swimming pools,
rinks,
cemeteries:

does not show, however,
houses, gardens, trees,
the Star-Phoenix Office,
the naval barracks,
old women out with shopping baskets,
children on a merry-go-round
or riding the toy train
in Kinsmen's Park.

LIFE IS A FLOWING

Life you said
is a flowing
contains death

Yesterday
I heard you had died.
A great stone
blocks the current.
Only the smallest trickle
of living
water
can pass

though it boils up
angrily
against the stone.

Outside my window
the leaves ripple in the wind.
Midsummer
is over.

From now on
the days will grow
shorter.

Life is a flowing
Life is

death is
life
flowing

THE HERO AS ESCAPE ARTIST

On the prairie the folk hero is Louis Riel
coming to grips with those Eastern bastards
and finally being hanged by them.
In Ontario, I suppose it's his arch-enemy
the victorious Scot old John A.
with a whisky bottle in one pocket
and the CPR's Last Spike in the other.

In New Brunswick, though (at least in King's County)
the hero is neither Victor nor Victim
but the Escape Artist, the Convict Houdini,
Henry More Smith
(alias Frederick Henry More)
tailor, pedlar, burglar, horse-thief
and theatrical showman.

Condemned to death in 1814
for stealing a black horse
(on which he had escaped from an earlier burglary)
he lay on a sickbed in a cold prison.
The kindhearted son of the sheriff,
who thought he was dying,
left the door of the cell open
while he went to fetch hot bricks
to warm the prisoner's bed

but when he came back
with the bricks, wrapped in paper,
and his foolish smile
the prisoner was gone,
walking past the room
where the sheriff and the parson
sat talking together,
and through the locked front door.

Captured again, he was watched more closely,
but disappeared from successive prisons,
broke chains, handcuffs, neck collars,
an iron staple
that fastened him to the floor.
(Where did he get the strength,
on a diet of one pound of bread a day
and a little water?)

Stayed long enough
in the King's County Gaol
to entertain his captors with a puppet show
in which the mighty Buonaparte
was overcome by a Highlander
with a carved wooden head.

On the walls of his prison
he drew coloured pictures
which observers later insisted
danced along with the puppets
when this Mysterious Stranger
played his flute.

A mesmerizer and magician,
maybe the Devil himself
(some people spoke of
his flashing eyes
as pools of black fire)
yet he read the Bible
and quoted it to the magistrates

("If any man seem wise
let him become a fool")

Having been pardoned (an anticlimax)
he could not resist
stealing a pair of earrings

was imprisoned again
but escaped this time
across the border into Maine

dropping casually
as he ran
the chains, the handcuffs,
the stray notes of his flute.

THE LIVING GOD

Waking up, I remember
not my own dream
(whatever it was)
but that dream of Jung's
in which God sits on a golden throne
above a cathedral
and lets drop on it
a tremendous turd.

Why did Jung not think the dream funny?
Surely, God as Victorian papa
reading his newspaper after breakfast
sitting on his throne
is rather a joke;
or is he the naughty small boy,
grown to be Almighty,
out of pure mischief
defacing Papa's universe?

Jung thought it a true vision
of the divine,
and maybe it was.
Hurricanes may be only
the winds of god's indigestion;
what we smell
rotten in the world

may be the stench of the divine
privy as well as our own.
Some mornings, hearing the news, I wonder
what has God eaten
(after all, he is behind the headlines,
since he created
the devil and us).

Still, I don't blame him.
Even God must be bored sometimes
hearing those holy, holy, holy hymns
and all those sermons
congratulating him on his justice and mercy.
He must sometimes want to be
a devil of a fellow
having a high old time
painting the universe red
and black,
killing a few enemies
and friends
with the blow of one hand
(a thunderbolt
or other Act of God)

and after
eating and drinking too much
grossly
shitting on the world.

IS THE PATHETIC FALLACY TRUE?

When I was a child
the stones were living.
Hot under my hand, they felt like flesh,
and sands slipped through my fingers
with a caress.

Yes, everything was alive:

the clumsy, roaring wind
stepped on the flounced pink dress
of the apple-tree,
tearing it to shreds

the puffed cheeks of clouds

the brook with its pebbled tongue
and the hoarse old grave old sea
its gravelly song

and earth itself
a brown warm girl
turning and tanning in the sun.

All false, all wrong,
somebody told me:
Winds are not lovers,
clumsy or gentle.
There's no blood
in stones,
no tears in water.

Nevertheless
sometimes lately when I touch a chair or table
I think I feel atoms stir
under my fingers

and at night in dreams I hear
the small remote voices of grains of dust
or the inaudible whispers of stars

as they will speak to me some time
when I lie with the living grass above me
and the wind my old lover
singing me to sleep

and to wake

METAMORPHOSIS

I dreamed a lady came
while I lay dreaming
and slipped inside my skin.
She pushed her hands
her long distorted hands
where mine should be.

I was a child.
I sat on the back step of my grandmother's house
and dreamed my grandmother
slipped into my skin.

I was old as the hills
(what hills? The hills behind the house).
I grasped my grandmother's cane
I breathed her breath.

I dreamed a lady came
while I was sleeping
and changed herself to me.
Now I protest
these long hands with their twining fingers.
Not mine.

These are not mine, these eyes.

I will wash off this skin.

EACH JOURNAL AN I-LAND

Journals are written by lonely people,
L.M. Montgomery knew
(lonely, though she never lived alone).

Were you a kindred spirit, Maud?

You loved your Island:
sea, rocks, sand-dunes, dulse,
sloping fields of buttercups,
of fat red clover
of more delicate white,
of caraway frothing up
like tides.

You loved Herman Leard,
the young farmer you thought not worthy of you,
whose ungrammatical letters
saying nothing special
you kept under your pillow, wept over,
knew by heart
before he died young.

You loved Penzie Macneill,
your girl schoolmate
who also died young;

loved your father, who neglected you,
might, if she had lived, have loved your mother,
whose funeral was your first memory
(cold touch of her face
when you kissed her in the coffin)
did not much love your grandparents Macneill
though they did their duty by you
and you by them

certainly did not love your stepmother
sharp-tongued and jealous
or her home in Prince Albert, Saskatchewan

did not love conceited young Edwin Simpson
to whom you were engaged for a time,
probably did not much love Ewen Macdonald,
your Presbyterian parson of a husband, terrified of hell.

I hope you loved your sons.

You loved your upper room in the grandparents' house,
with its plants and pictures and bookcases
                                                            loved books
even Gibbon's *Decline and Fall of the Roman Empire*
loved reading the dictionary
loved to write letters
loved your journal

maybe sometimes loved
those girls you created:
Anne, Emily, Kilmeny
loved your cat Daffy,
even though he killed squirrels,
which you also loved.

You loved a garden,
picking out seeds from the catalogue,
getting your hands in the earth,
seeing something grow
that you had planted.

You loved the woods:
"How I love trees,"
you wrote.
"Often and often
when I am alone in the woods
I will put my arms tenderly
about some old, grey-lichened trunk
and press my face to it."

Makes me remember
when I was a child
in spring
embracing an apple-tree
or kneeling to kiss
the moist black soil
of a fresh-ploughed field

waiting for seeds.

Dennis Cooley

IN HIS TANGERINE SKIN

we buried him
in mint condition
on his eyes
two georges
they shone like hens eggs
he inhaled the dark
hhhhgg hhggg
engorged it
like a badger breathing
for blood
when we shovelled him in
christ he was a gorgeous man
the eyes were breathing
& shining blood

THE END OF THE LINE

reached out to send you this line
out to send you this line reached
to send you this line reached out
send you this line reached out to
you this line reached out to send
this line reached out to send you
line reached out to send you this

FREEZE UP

                                        a few pebbles of
        rain red dust & the
creak of hinges   working hard   & dark cracks
    open   cranks its shutters   open & will
                        not close for the night

                                under the streetlights
                                dark drinks the light
                                you can see its breath
                                horses at lightpoles
                                stamping like ghosts

over night frost soakd in railway tracks
chains of it jangle gardens
tangle the tomatoes in steel

inside night
vertebrae hang from our neck
on wires of winter

am a tingle in dawn now
taps on your window
panes on the blankets
a bleeding of white
where you have lain

frost in morning snaps on
electric in dawn

when dark drank the light
from your hand

GYPSOPHILA

now
the new snow brightens
my window deepens
lays it light
upon the ground
the grass below
that holds it gasgreen
into the yellow warmth
in early November
seeds tighten/flare
under this skin of
snow singing
a billion glass suns
in the night
) remembering
Penny Lyn
her gypsophila
in our garden
puffs of gypsophila
white vapour
blown
around the orange
burn of marigolds

when in August the ochre
ate its way
scalding thru the
window of my room
& you bathd/breathd in
the slick white acid
inside untoucht
that moment
cool & still
inside the bed

here
in the mellow spill
of sunfall
the wax spaces
tell me
you are gone
Nov 8
your letter says
Toronto
out of the tinbarn box clicks
) the winter dreaming
at my door
the words that have not come
dont take my words love lightly
your voice tells
of the quick
cells rising
flicker
cells your body carries
growing
dividing &
growing
growing & dividing
us now
you now
these 2000 miles
a child's breath away

THE LOVE SONG OF J L KRAFCHENKO OR THE TRANS CANADA IN (TRANCE CRYPT

crossing

hhhoo   yyyooooooooooo   hhoo   yyYoooOOooOOOO

pooshka   poosh ka   pooshka

---

po   o   sh   ka   po   os hk a

HOO

train at the level

coupling

ooshka pooShka pOoshKA PoSHkA POSHkA

end for end

poo sh ka Poo SH kA POO SH K A POOSH KA

YOOOOOOOOOOOO OOOOOOO

BY THE RED

by the red river
river so low
walk by the willows
feel the rains blow

feel the slow rains dear
feel the rains flow
september morning
cold rain like snow

if you cant call now
call when you can
warm in your voice love
glad in your hands

you at my window
you at my door
hold me once more dear
hold me once more

leave you a letter
leave you this song
leave you my love dear
sayin so long

send me some words though
though they are numb
words to remember
when they will come

willows of green leaves
sprinklers of sun
spindles of air love
whiskey of sun

crow in a door dear
crow in a door
hungry for somethin
wont see you no more

so pay me no visit
pay me no heed
sun starts to rise
sun starts to bleed

headingly jail love
headingly jail
think of me penny
in headingly jail

by the red river
river so low
walk by the willows
blowin in snow

JAZZ

when he came upon her
(crow crowding light)
a whirr of flesh
naked there in the fields
wet with insects her voice
drizzling in dry air & the elms
choked with fire & heat
dumped into dogs

could she read his lips did she
put his lips to her
ear spill his honey words
into her did she gasp
wrinkled from grass & twigs
in that tingle of time

did she grasp/wildly
what he uttered the new conception
by word of mouth that crept up
on her did she pause
overcome with shiver
of saxophone breath
within her ear
nerves & tremblings
the very tips of her skin
did she think
she could carry it
off shaken with what he sang

& afterward the sweet whisper
of sweat & spittle in her ear

& a breeze strolls by &
a sperm of necklace
: cool on her

adam all ears
eves dropping when he comes
upon her & she in morning
hangs night out to dry

PRAIRIE VERNACULAR

what they edited in fall
left footprints where (the land
parched) rocks had stood & thot

inside overshoes of winter
under buckles of bins & barns
boots of pig pens
seeds peeped beneath breath
hid in hides with stacks of bones
that slept & dreamt of cabbage & corn

all winter long under the pages
under snow & ice spring rehearsed
small creatures waited for march
to ransack their rooms

each spring they ruled the land
like foolscap those farmers
laconic as typewriters
scraped its face free
from the fat of winter
from the water marks
spring left in its pressing

& then there is a certain
slant of light thats pencil-
sharpened to a tightness   in the grass

& august men come to kneel
& read what is written there
thousands of grains at their finger
tips they poured into the earth
till it was green with noise

bent &   watched over them
till   /combining in fall   :
: the first   :   : stammer
:   rattling   in the hopper
then:
the heavy pour

till we were sunburnt
/with words/
fluent with them

in the fullness of light   the fullness of time

BEHIND THE DOOR

bodies preferred to think of themselves
crowding cheek by jowl
into barns jewelled with grain
heavy hay & a farmer to keep them
warm & fed to bring them newly
born into rooms of horn & hoof
rut and root rain on the roof
of their brains

"to keep seed alive upon the face of all the earth"

animals
girdled in the cluck
& moon of milk
egg white of cat & pigeon
eyeblink & heartslump
animals were muscles
made throatnoises through the lump
of months

secret in the stomach of wood

they arced or folded
in ecstasy eyes
flooded with oil
when the farmer touched them
nuzzled their chins & udders
in winter
inside ribs of wood
pails of water

spoke to them
language of grass & sun
what in the nights that are long
husbands to wives say
of grass & sun

& the opening of gates
of summer in them
the way water sits when it is almost ice

animals were leather
the farmer wore
close to his heart

they were
pouches filled with tobacco
in his dream
vests he wore to church

at night they spoke silently
to one another
the bodies dangled like babies
in the hump of barn

standing & standing in puddles of time

weight of nights wet
as sand

& when January punched at them
sandbagged snow against their eyes
they lay down into the sweet
grunt of straw that melodied dreams
hidden in hides

the paunch of dark
the lazy lift of time
left like smoke in the crease of dreams

all that long waiting

bodies were blood in a barn of bone

TREES IN WINTER

furious	winter
winter	stiff
powder	their
in waiting	water
green water	trees
shakes	waiting
the dreaming	power
sun alive	in alive
detonates	dreams their
trees	shaken
their	green of water
sun power	furious
water	dreaming the
stiff power	pour of sun
pour of dream	detonating them
their	powder

detonating them	their
pour of sun	pour of dream
the dreaming	stiff power
furious	water
green water	sun power
wading	wading
their dream	their
alive in	trees
power	powder
waiting	detonates
water	sun alive
snow	the dreaming
trees	green water
their	in waiting
winter	winter
stiff	furious

POLICE INFORMER

I got this leather jacket see
a black one   right
its like a cop jacket
only a little slicker   I like to think
one a   those American ones   I guess yd say
            you know   Hill Street Blues
look a lot like Billy donja think

so anyways   I just got this jacket eh
& the women they like it man
                a lot
its really soft & a bit puffy
              a winter one eh
so the women all want to touch it like
        so thats   ok with me
                  I don mind
they can do   all the touching they want

but one time   one of the women
she reaches across
like Im just talking to her   right
were havin a coffee   & she
reaches across & touches the shoulder
& she says   get this   she says
c'ni see yr night stick   huh
that's what she said
lemme see
yr night stick

ok

GRAVITY

have felt stars swarm my face
my heart swim in my hand have
heard what Newton said the greater
the mass the stronger the pull
the further the distance the less attraction

know only i am in a stone
I am a stone
a child swings round &
round as a moon a child tugs
from far away holds me here
keeps my thoughts
from swarming
from flying off

my daughter on the other end
the cord stronger than gravity
feel the cord how it vibrates,
heart in my hand

THIS ONLY WORLD

what I remember most -the silence
most of all an enormous silence
unlike any I have ever known
and we would listen the way you listen
to a baby in its crib and you fear
it is not alive or breathing
and you cannot hear for the longest time

silence so vast and deep I begin to hear
my own body the swish in the vessels
my heart I can hardly believe
the muscles move and there is
the rustle shirts and vests

make when you are dressing
in morning I hear them rubbing
when they move over each other
the way we move our silence

settlers I have heard on the Canadian prairie
moved into a huge silence wavered
on air there like birds in a desert
& emptiness not to be believed
tumbled past

and the stars my god the stars far more
than ever I would have thought
I do not know what but this sky
is so black a deep black but it is
bright with sun the earth is

a small bright light so breath
-takingly blue & white its
gentle cloud of breath
dear earth dear child
so all alone the home we left
the earth so round I never knew
how round how small
until I saw the earth

DRIED APRICOTS

dried apricots we found dried apricots today
and I thought when I was young
I would watch the moon and that's what
I thought the moon is a dried apricot

my mother would say that's nice Aleksandrov
and she would tell me stories there would be
snow and cold at the door
you would drink or smells of gardens
in spring when everything's wet from rain
and you get stuck once in your rubber boots
and she pulls you out, scolding

once she said Aleksandr look and there was
a small bird in her hand a robin I think
or a yellow bird so bright I thought
it was the sun there my mother held in her hand

and now this bag of little moons
some friend has smuggled onto the ship
it's as if we are closer to home
earth whirls in fluff and deserts red as icing
giant eye balls swirl to tropical storms
I have never been to but something happens
when there is ice laid on a teal
table clean as mother's linen in Hudson Bay
and Moscow and it is winter

thunder rain the singing of birds the earth turning
green under us and blue blue as Anishka's eyes

all this seems now so very far away
as if it happened a long time ago
"and we no longer there
and it is not known
when we will be again"

Lorna Crozier

YOU'RE SO COVERED WITH SCARS

You're so covered with scars
you forget where they come from.
Like birds they sing to the wounded
who descend from the railings of bridges
to follow you. In bars the cripples limp
to your table, drag their bleeding casts
towards the criss-cross of your face.
The old sit beside you in stations,
cough their lives into your lap. And now
I have crawled from under your bed to lie
against you. I trace the braille of your body:
the broken lip, the hole in the side
of your face. But you are emptied of stories.
Instead you press into my skin. The scars
cover me like feathers.

MARRIAGE: GETTING USED TO

It did not take me long
to get used to his leather
wings, no, they felt good
like an old, much-loved coat
draped over my shoulders
It was his feet I couldn't stand,
his horny feet, ugly as a bird's,
the yellow claws and the pride
he took in them:

how he oiled the scales
and saved the clippings
making me a necklace
from the broken claws
sewing flakes of skin
like sequins in my clothes

Even his tricks were okay
the way his words turned
to flames at parties
sizzling flies from the air,
lighting cigarettes for ladies
with his tongue. It wasn't that
that bothered me.

It was waking to find him
with a flashlight and a mirror
staring under the covers at his feet
It was his nails
clicking across linoleum
(he was too vain to wear slippers)
and after he had gone to work,
it was the fallen gold scales
that lay on the sheet like scattered coins

THE FAT LADY'S DANCE

The fat lady can't get out of bed.
He has done it before, his idea of a joke.
He has left her there and gone to work
after he has watched each greasy egg
slither down her throat, after he has made her
swallow every wad of buttered bread.

When she hears the door close, she snivels,
she starts to cry as she always does.
But something strange begins to happen.
Somewhere under the globs of flesh
she feels a motion, a memory of movement.
The fat lady thinks of feet.
She stops crying,
opens her mouth, sucks in all
the rage her belly can hold.
With a massive heave-ho she rolls
off the bed to the floor and goes on rolling
splits the door frame with her legs
crumbles the wall with her shoulders
crashes through the living room
onto the steps and rolls down the street.

Cars skid out of her way,
she carooms off a bus
and on she rolls, her flesh
slaps the pavement,
children follow her booming parade,
dogs bark at her one piece band.
She fells trees, she bursts hydrants
she rolls through the town
and up to the door of his office.
With one great yell, one mighty heave
she rolls the building flat
then rises up on jiggling legs
and shaking the brick dust off her nightgown
she pirouettes out of town.

THIS ONE'S FOR YOU

Hey, big hummer,
who can strut like you?
Crotch-tight jeans, boots
shiny as pool balls, heels
pounding stars into pavement
you call sky.

Hey, big rooster,
who can cockadoodledo
like you do? You raise the
bloody sun from his corner
your voice, brass
bell in the ring.

Hey, prize fighter,
who can screw like you?
Women howl your name,
say no man will take
your place, buzz them
like an electric drill.
You spin the world
on the end of your cock.

Hey, big talker,
waited all my life
for a man like you.
Come my way, I'll blow
the fuses in your big machine,
short all your circuits.
I'll break the balls
you rack on the table,
I'll bust your pool cue.

THE FOETUS DREAMS

1

Lungs.
It dreams heart.
Spleen. Liver.
It dreams two faces:

one it will wear
before it is born.

2

In the morning
the foetus dreams the sun.
It pushes against red walls
wanting to touch light
with pale buds of fingers.

There is no sun.

The foetus dreams
the shadow of a cloud
bruises its eyelids.
It hears rain
tapping on the forehead
of its mother.
It dreams
it is a fish that swims
in her laughter
through the seasons
of her blood.

3

The foetus dreams
wind fills its skin-bag,
lifts it out and up

an ocular *o*

round and clear
as a bubble blown
from a child's ring.

The earth shrinks
to a speck of dust
under a new-formed nail.
Stars like fireflies
catch in its fine
black hair.

4

The foetus dreams
it is a whisper
sealed in a clear jar
set on a kitchen shelf
where a red geranium
presses its petals
against glass skin
until night turns
the window cold and dark.

5

The foetus dreams a man
hangs a moonstone around its mother's throat.

It dreams a man
follows her through the shadows of the park,

stands outside her bedroom window,
leaves his breath in circles on the pane.

It dreams a man with a face it has known
moves his mouth in words across her belly.

It cries and kicks
                    the voice away
beating the stretched skin like a drum.

6

The foetus dreams a name
it fills like a round
glass or a mouth.
It moves like light
into the spaces defined
by the letters. It moves
like breath into the spaces
between the letters.

It grows within the name
as ice expands in stone
fissures
            yet the stone holds
and will not break.

7

The foetus dreams it is
a black hole
            cut into the tinny blue.
It dreams someone
cuts off its foot for a dime,
someone splits its tongue
so it can say a word. It dreams
it sits on its mother's hip
while she lies sleeping. In the dawn
it flies away
                with her black
and dreaming eyes.

8

It dreams it is a mouth,
a fish swimming in a mouth.
It dreams its mother
hooks a fish.
She reels it in
on a long thin vein
she winds
round and round her wrist.

DROUGHT

The hawk sits on the post,
head tucked in his shoulder.
It is mid-day. He knows the sun,
if he took flight, would singe
his wings and burn the moisture
from his eyes. Around him mice
crackle through the yellow grass,
their bodies small flames. Gophers
driven by the memory of seeds
move from darkness.

The hawk sleeps,
head tucked in his shoulder.
Soon he must hunt,
slice his wings through heat
that beats like rain
on the dry earth. His shadow
will offer the small
            a moment's respite
before he drops and drinks.

LOON SONG

The loon has left its voice
and flown away.
I hear it in the early light
and just before sleeping,
rolling through reeds towards the shore.

It lives in the lake
and sometimes in the mind.
Now it sits in the belly
of a rainbow trout
moving like memory through darkness.

If you can empty yourself,
lay your senses around you
like five white cups,
it will build a nest in one of them.

You will see the distances
only birds know, feel the loneliness
that rose from the long dark throat
before the loon, weary of its voice,
flew away.

CABBAGES

Long-living and slow,
content to dream in the sun,
heads tucked in, cabbages
ignore the caress of the
cabbage butterfly, the soft
sliding belly of the worm.

You know it's crazy
but they lie so still,
so self-contained, you imagine them
laying eggs
in the earth's dark pockets,
expect one morning they'll be gone,
dragging themselves
to the creek behind the house,

making their way
with great deliberation
to the sea.

POTATOES

No one knows
what potatoes do.
Quiet and secretive
they stick together.
So many under one roof
there is talk of incest.

The pale, dumb faces,
the blank expressions.
Potato dumplings.
Potato pancakes.
Potato head.

In dark cellars
they reach across the potato bin
to hold one another
in their thin white arms.

ZUCCHINI

The zucchini strokes the slim waists
of the pea vines, peeks under
the skirts of the yellow beans,
squares its shoulders and says to the rhubarb,
There's only room for one of us.

But mainly it is passive,
a voyeur lying still and silent
in its speckled lizard skin.

In secret shadows it spreads
like must over the garden,
the zucchini's eyes are open all night.

THE OLDEST SONG

The hens in the dusty twilight of the chicken coop
sing in strange low voices, not the squawking
we think we know, for that is what they do
when we are near. Weird sisters these, all white
the dance they do while the woman sleeps.
Her own small egg, perhaps her last, travels
the dark to its inland sea. Heads swaying from
side to side, the hens all lift one foot, pause,
before they set it down as if it were the first
time they touched the ground, here only for one night,
so white, they could have fallen from the moon.
The woman sinks into feathers, into her own
dark dreams. That part of her that walks in sleep
and won't remember in the sun's first light
wonders at the voices her body moves toward,
the hens singing their oldest song
while strings of moonstones
grow warm inside them.

WITHOUT HANDS

(In memory of Victor Jara, the Chilean musician whose hands were smashed by the military to stop him from playing his guitar and singing for his fellow prisoners in the Santiago stadium. Along with thousands of others, he was tortured and finally killed there in September, 1973.)

All the machines in the world
stop. The textile machines, the paper machines,
the machines in the mines turning stones to fire.
Without hands to touch them, spoons, forks and knives
forget their names and uses, the baby is not bathed,
bread rises on the stove, overflows the bowl.
Without hands, the looms
stop. The music
                        stops.
The plums turn sweet and sticky and gather flies.

Without hands
                        without those beautiful conjunctions
those translators of skin, bone, hair
two eyes go blind
two pale hounds sniffing ahead and doubling back
to tell us
            of hot and cold or the silk of roses after rain
are lost
            two terns feeling the air in every feather
are shot down.

Without hands my father doesn't plant potatoes
row on row, build a house for wrens,
or carry me
from the car to bed
when I pretend I'm sleeping.
On wash-days my mother doesn't hang clothes
on the line, she doesn't turn the pages of a book
and read out loud,
to teach me how to lace my shoes.

Without hands my small grandmother
doesn't pluck the chicken for our Sunday meal
or every evening, before she goes to sleep,
brush and brush her long white hair.

OVERTURE

O penis,
apostrophe of lust,
come out of the cage
where you lie sleeping.

O snow leopard,
lithe and rare,
when you raise your head,
the birds tremble in the trees,
are struck
            like wooden matches,
flames falling around you
feather by feather.

O cock of the walk,
O proud rooster who struts his stuff,
come near.
Your comb is carnelian and brilliant,
I want to wear it in my hair,
I want to put it to my lips
and with tongue and tissue
play you
your favourite song.

O prick of delight,
O word made flesh,
I turn out all the lights
so I can hear you.

EGGS

Mary won't eat chicken
because she dreamed a hen
with her daughter's head
spoke to her.

She takes this for an omen
and why not? What's more female
than a hen, its rosary of eggs
growing inside, each
a memory of self,
a first genesis, the yoke
spotted with blood—
an image held in our brains
before our birth.

There's something about chickens.
As a child I loved to clean them,
push my hand into the cavity
(like the space I knew
inside me) pull out the guts,
the heart, the gizzard with its stones,
the tiny eggs warm in my palm.

Nothing was like the diagrams
in our health texts in school.
In the kitchen there was shit
if the skin of the intestines broke
and always there was blood.

The blood that made me
bend in pain
was a secret no one talked about.
Then I was the daughter.
                                        My head
separate from my body
knew more of a chicken's
than my own.

ON THE SEVENTH DAY

On the first day God said
Let there be light.
And there was light.
On the second day
God said, *Let there be light,*
and there was more light.

What are you doing? asked God's wife,
knowing he was the dreamy sort.
You created light yesterday.

I forgot, God said. *What can I do*
about it now?

Nothing, said his wife.
But pay attention!
And in a huff she left
to do the many chores
a wife must do in the vast
(though dustless) rooms of heaven.

On the third day God said
Let there be light. And
on the fourth and the fifth
(his wife off visiting his mother).

When she returned there was only
the sixth day left. The light
was so blinding, so dazzling
God had to stretch and stretch the sky to hold it
and the sky took up all the room—
it was bigger than anything
even God could imagine.
Quick, his wife said,
make something to stand on!
God cried, *Let there be earth!*

and a thin line of soil
nudged against the sky like a run-over serpent
bearing all the blue in the world on its back.

On the seventh day God rested
as he always did. Well, *rest*
wasn't exactly the right word,
his wife had to admit.

On the seventh day God
went into his study
and wrote in his journal
in huge curlicues and loops
and large crosses on the *t*'s
changing all the facts, of course,
even creating Woman
from a Man's rib, imagine that!
But why be upset? she thought.
Who's going to believe it?

Anyway, she had her work to do.
Everything he'd forgotten
she had to create
with only a day left to do it.
Leaf by leaf,
paw by paw, two by two,
and now nothing
could be immortal
as in the original plan.

Go out and multiply, yes,
she'd have to say it,
but there was too little room for
life without end,
forever and ever,
always, eternal, *ad infinitum*
on that thin spit of earth
under that huge prairie sky.

E.F. Dyck

S/HE

1. daddy says her feet are gunboats
                        her ankles are thick
                        her lessons cost too much
                        when will I find time
                        to pick my toes
and he lets her get away
            with nothing
makes her feel basically/well
unwanted uncouth unloved
unlike jane russell and her big
tits or heddy lamarr and her classy
waist or the movies' stars and their trim
legs on the silver screen in dysart
nobody has any class just a bunch
of ukes I think I'll change my name
trim my moustache and practise
my baritone, ladies, here I come

& she looked for daddy in the grass
in the sky in the slough in the willow
found him not & made him up
perfect daddy with accent
weary of travel & who chose to build
upon the ruins of dysart where he found
a crocus mauve & fragile on a sandy ridge
in the parkland

2. mummy says this little boy is smart
this little boy is good
this little boy is destined
this little boy whacks off
whack him daddy
and she lets him get away
with anything
makes him feel like a missionary
who will save the world
not like daddy who sulks & ruts
upon her belly stretched by past
& future brothers & sisters
serve god/down with rum
up with jesus
save us all from sin
here in turnhill where the river
runs through the breaks & the day
hangs like judgement over the hills
which in turn remind that little boy
of his sister's breasts but he mustn't
do it anymore it will fall off & then
the mission board won't send him afield
& who will serve when uncle john is gone
o god o god o gog o gog o gag

3. & the birth of poetry
for the first time
they're in love & do it
for love only love only
it doesn't last the fresh smell
the pure language the first
poem

begins at once the destructive process
of growth & the derivations
she was got with child
        your problem my problem
        our problem their problem
        why didn't you do this why
        didn't you do that why
        didn't it fall off why
        did it happen   let's
        kill it

4. after that it was easy
to see that they were totally
mismatched & with practise
to make the marriage work
& no play
missionaries don't play in the hay
crocuses don't grow in the hay
hay is not essential to the argument
which by now is so perfectly known
it can be run by in segments or
backward for variety or in code
it's so important   more than
& forever

5. dear reader, these hypotheses
tragic & comic if in us inducing
pity & terror & pitiless laughter
have yet not served their purposes
have not unleashed the alchemy
her coiling tiger, his fuming dragon

AT STUD

for R.C.

I'll never forget Kornelson
riding his pinto stud
into my father's yard
his muscles working
under his thin cheeks
        where is she? he yelled
        from the saddle/the pinto
        lunging toward the barn

Stay in the house said my father
help mum with the dishes
        in the barn, he yelled back
& Kornelson dismounted/the stud
fully aroused & they fought
each other to the door

I knew she was standing
spread-legged in her stall
creamy and swollen
we never rode her in heat
& when I heard the door
the door opening to the pasture
& when I heard easy girl atta girl
I was running for the barn
I was riding & her haunches working
under me/the heat of her through me

tie her head down said Kornelson
up there so her forelegs are higher
& she won't kick & get a sack

The pinto reared & I saw
his piebald penis/a white splotch
on a musky tube as thick and long
as my arm
            Kornelson hauled him down
            pulled his leather gloves on
            don't need oil said my father
            here said Kornelson, lead him
            behind her & give him his head

The smashing weight of the stud
caught her on the rump
the stud sprang forward
            shit yelled Kornelson
            pull him back/I'm too low
my father jerked the pinto
back & Kornelson's leather hands
raised the glistening penis
to that creamy slit & she
screamed at his thrust
it went all the way in/the shit
flew   as the stud arched and shuddered
arched & shuddered   then slid
down & out & she stood/a sack
over her tied-down head
& her legs apart
            it's done said Kornelson
            as he slapped a wet glove
            on his long hard thigh
            yup said my father what
            do I owe you?

I'll never forget Kornelson
riding the Turnhill stud
out of my father's yard

riding my small boy's dream
out of my father's yard

EXPERIMENTS IN GRAMMAR

Poet
learn by experiments/grammar
the art of true & well speaking
your language
thus your accidents (as writing)
your poems
will tell/precisely

1. morphology
choose a morpheme
e.g. ball &
affix to it/endings   thus
balls   balling   balled
        the rules tell us nothing
        of vulgarity
or ballerina
        her body catapults
        beyond morphology

from this conclude
that concatenation & the possibility
of iteration are not enough
for the compounding of words
(the sound of roundness &
the semantics of sphericity
intrude in the experiment)

yet/goethe's discovery
        the intermaxillary bone
        in the jaw of man
this   too   is morphology

2. phonology
hark/the sounds of words
do they imitate & what
or why no arrested cough?

consider the beginnings
the worship of gods by liturgies of vowels
& the ideas within consonants

choice   too
for we do not include e.g.
nggoynggoynggoythankyou
though the instruments
are identical

suppose a race of mutes
& their written language
                    what grammar?
or write a poem of sounds/only
transrational & very near
                    let go/cough

3. syntax
the generation of sentences
well-formed & infinite in number
as described in the sutras

as invented by children
speaking in predicates
(for the subject is understood)

till/in schools the nominative
is forced upon them driving
inwards the first grammar

& we older   talk to ourselves
in predicates   as children
our inner speech

the task is to recover
the grammar within

i.e. having written/strike out
all names of things/leave in
all properties & actions &
study their energy
your grammar

4. semantics
how to understand the meanings
of words except by/finally
the pointed finger & the mime?

no ideas but in things/yet
a ball/alone is unimaginable
& no conception fails to invoke
the universe

no not things relations
the thrust & parry of the verb
the invitation to dance & the power
of ambiguity/its call
to completeness

can we know
only by metaphor
species to genus
genus to species
& by proportion?

to experiment
is to construct
your equation

5. post experimentum
as hypotheses/all grammars leak
& buckets
invented in abbeys by hermits
we dip & dribble

try a new pail
there are only speech acts
which are doings

to do is to be
to be is to do
to-be-do-be-do

VI MOSSBANK: THE THIRTIES

41. The maharajah of Mossbank built *Missouri Farm*
Give me cream! *:Give me tea!*
he said to Jong *I'll call you Curley, eh?*
Yup, bought another section of land today!
Jong served the prince his milky lukewarm tea
and thought of warfare off the China Sea

42. In the year of the Long March in China
one of twenty leavings Kiangsi lived to cross
the River of Golden Sand:the chained bridge of Tatu
the Great Snow Mountain:the high Grasslands of Chiangsi
In the year of the Long March in Mossbank
a store burned down :ruined the Jew who ran it

43. Jewed him down :that dirty Jew
By the waters of Mossbank I sat and wept
Plucked his harp :jew-boy joe-boy
Jew go home :worse than a Chink
Chink is yellow :Jew is black
By the waters of Mossbank I sat and wept

44. The snows fell on the caves of Yenan
snow of millet :snow of wheat
snow of pepper :snow of sugar
snow of apple :snow of corn
snow of lice :snow of dust
The snows fell on the White Dove Cafe

45\. And a letter fell :on the White Dove Cafe
The children of Mossbank played with the children
of the sons or sons of relatives of the proprietors
of the White Dove Cafe as Jong read the letter
You must choose a name for your son
Your son who was born in Kwantung

46\. Many man has never known he has a son
On the Long March :many sons were lost
lost to peasants :lost to war
but in Mossbank :a son was found
His blue eyes shone in the prairie sun
His blond curly hair blew in the wind

47\. The sons differed but the father did not
He takka mirik :smurra butta
Customers got used to the son in the cafe
smiled at Jong :smiling at the boy
feeding him bars :cracking him a pop
He is a son for my son born in Kwantung

48\. Outside Toishan :rice was green
Outside Mossbank :wheat was brown
In the cafe the maharajah sipped his tea
He thought of war and thought of money
Jong fed a blue-eyed boy bars and pop
and thought of a son whose eyes were black

Patrick Friesen

TERRAIN

in thrall to the roots,
perennial in their mode,
I find the constant windflower
easily abandoning its petals.

this land is daubed with ashen easters,
with blue-eyed grass and goldenrod.

there is something vague in the colour,
something explicit in the form.

fire-confirmed and tree-broken,
this land holds the valerian edible
along the railroad, along the marsh;
the birdsfoot violet in the churchyard.

and yes, in thrall to the oak
and all divining months
when I hardened in grandfather's desert
of thistle, stone and snakeroot.

SOME KIND OF MEMORY

blood is not thickest
when we kiss deeply
but it swells full
when the veins carry
the echo of father footsteps
and winter horses
startled at their drinking

WINGS

the trees have taken on flesh

leaves curl around each last sound
and hold them unheard
until they fall to earth

(how could that whispering giant
dropping in the dark
hold such a clamour   such surprise)

the bone field is littered with the machine
and clothes once worn by angels

ragweed prevails
though hewn here and there by wings

the rain has softened
over the broken husk of a straying world
amid the sizzle of blue fires and the mist
fall's turning breathes

leaves draw blood   dropping
they release silence
like smoke in the purple weed

SUMMER GOING ON FALL

a heap of cement blocks
and a garden beside them

my barefoot daughter
eats apples off the ground
and sings an old story

the willow leaves are sticky
from last night's fogging
weeping birch too
and strawberries
and the oak out front

I swat at a fugitive mosquito
honing in suicidal as any zero combat plane

the sun is a hammer
driving my head down on my neck
until my eyes glaze over with the ache
and I sit in a buzzing tunnel
not moving

from somewhere my wife's voice says
no strawberries today
the bees must have fallen in the fog
no strawberries rest of the summer

and I say the effect couldn't be that fast

but then why no strawberries

my little girl's singing
about when she used to be a little girl
(she's only three
which seems young enough to me)

my wife points out the pruning she's done on the dogwood
and I notice through my haze
how japanese the dogwood looks
the intricacy of angles or something
maybe a thwarted kind of economy
whatever

the buzzing continues
and a cement truck rumbles by
with its space capsule turning
the foundations of another house within it

an acorn plummets
bouncing off the sidewalk into my lap
I crack it open
my wife says it's poison
I chew it anyway
birds eat them   why not me

and still my daughter singing

> I useta be happy
> I useta be mad
> I useta be happy
> so . . . that's what I had

and as if a carnegie hall of men
thrilled to every note and word
and she afloat on their applause

> thank you gentlemens

and the sun's got me
and the world's reeling
and it's christmas in my head

god rest her
god rest her   merry

CURLING AT ITS EDGES

curling at its edges
like paper   the yellowing moon
breaks when I touch it

like my red heart
like a leaf like dreams
the morning interrupts

I dream what was   apparently
a woman   almost thirty   hoeing weeds
a jar of water on a fencepost
her throat   as she drinks   a glass vase

and walking in a dream at noon   across the bridge
the white stroke of her arm
drops of water colliding silver with air
her hair dark and sleek   like an otter

eyes remember what was flesh
a dress brushing against russian thistles
shoes scuffing stones
a white finger bleeding from roses

I reach for the moon
to plant it like a seed
beside the porch   in the night
plant it and grow a sun
maybe   in the morning
a woman waking beside me

MY WIFE LIES QUIETLY

my wife lies quietly
so   just like we always did sleeping
yes   so beautiful   her shawl
roses on her black shawl
still   and still her violet eyes
and those worn hands   you wouldn't believe
how soft   soft   on my mouth
my eager mouth kissing   those fingers
those slender arms   those breasts

she moved with me   her hands on my hips
she twisted   we were so young   so
she twisted   spun on top of me   calling
Johann   Johann   she called me   she found me
yes   called in the night   through the whole world

we lay awake together
as winter tried to get in beneath the door
and that was long ago
we were young   even though
we were so young
things weren't always like that

I WASN'T THINKING OF THE CHILD

I wasn't thinking of the child
swimming in the stone shell of her belly

I remembered cattle
how they lowed uneasily in labour
how scrawny legs stuck out like branches
how father tugged
as if he might tear the calf apart
how things were born   no matter what

no ceremony

only the animal butting into sight

I remembered smells
camphor or the slough
where the new one splashed bawling like a calf

I remember the infant her lank prince
animal or fish
wriggled at her breast
waiting pale-eyed for the waking kiss

PA POEM 6: AMONG THE GLADS

when the pain got bad pa's nerves went
couldn't endure squabbles at the table
he'd leave pale and sweating for the garden
where he'd kneel among the glads and go through his ritual
whatever it was he did touching or stroking stems
something to soothe him I guess assure himself he was really there

and sometimes he'd strike out with an uncoiling rage
hit my brother once with his belt gouged flesh with the buckle
an accident pure and simple he never thought of the metal
but it was a rage that made ma speak out
it must have scared her to make her turn on pa like that
in front of the kids telling him he was wrong

what pa said or did after that I don't know
but I think the man must have holed up
probably in the basement standing near the furnace
wondering what it was he was doing
how he could flail one of his boys like that

and I'd be surprised if he wasn't remembering his dad
and whatever lay between them
the boy aching alone between steinbach and la broquerie
his mother something shadowy beneath blankets
slipping toward her death that night
words rasping in his father's throat
harrowing his life away in stone fields

grandpa and pa I could confuse those men if I thought too much
about them
and how he could thrash me as if I was someone else
he usually had control of himself
thrashed me in the basement for something I did
pa my dad teaching me across his knee
ma said it hurt him more than me it must have

PA POEM 7: REHEARSING FOR SUNDAY

pa sang real well
I used to hear him at home rehearsing for sunday
sometimes just him and ma sometimes with other people

ma played piano the others standing behind her
pa maybe sucking a couple of sen sens
and sometimes I'd be lying in bed almost asleep
and I'd hear ma's voice like glass or maybe water on glass
I'd forget the bad notes
and I'd listen past the melody and the harmony
right through to pa's voice
almost clear not quite like a cello with smoke at the edge
filling the spaces just when you realized they were there

that's it everyone else was singing to make those intervals
and pa letting them hang a bit just enough to make you want to
close them
then swooping in there as if that's the only thing could happen right then

pa sang real well
until his lungs went and then the last days his throat

one sunday he and I sat facing each other in the living room
his voice was hoarse I hoped he would clear it
but he didn't or couldn't and that harsh voice grew into stories
of his father and I thought he was forgiving him for something
though the dates were all wrong I wanted to hallow this dying
but I had not learned to sing

EASTER

it's time

children this is where easter happened
on this street at this tree
this poplar well I climbed it
and saw grandfather's pine miles away
and here on this lawn
one summer evening I heard the 'moonlight sonata'

I begin to shiver
there's always this danger of losing control
when I go back
when everything true stands before me
and there's no way of letting my children know
I just point out the objects

and maybe one day if I'm lucky
one of them remembers the tree
the way a breeze rustled leaves that day
how the old man stared at something not there

oh christ doesn't matter

father didn't show me where he stood
some days I make the rounds
remembering where I think I saw him
photos where he and the place are the same
I try to stand on his ground
wondering where the man was

I tear at boards
pull nails with my teeth
dismantle the house with all my might
toppling history on home street
to father digging the cellar in 1945
singing toward his wedding

what could keep him here
this earthly love

or not worshipping her body   loving her
or the garden   revealing
what couldn't be shown   what he could never say

I can say though that easter is here
that mom whistled my dog to the post here
that pa tied the dog here
that they slaughtered him here

I can say
that my birthday   each summer   is here
in this field
that I see how the world turns here
dawn to dusk

and this is it
how the world happens for me
this is the place
I am here
wherever I am I am
here

SUNDAY AFTERNOON

on sunday afternoons all the fathers in town slept
I think they dreamed of old days and death
sometimes you could hear them cry
the summer air was still at the window
flies on the screen and the radio playing softly in the kitchen

mother slid a fresh matrimonial cake onto potholders on the stove
picked up a book a true book of someone else's life
sunglasses a pitcher of lemonade and a straw hat
spread a blue blanket in the backyard near the lilac shrubs for shade
I lay down one ear hearing children in the garden
she never escaped all the way nor did she want to not quite
this much on a sunday afternoon went a long way

downtown boys rode main street toward fiery crashes they imagined
twisted wrecks with radios playing
rock'n'roll insulting the highway
townspeople gathered on the shoulder
standing as near as they could to the impossible moment between what's here and not

a girl's body sprawled in the ditch no one knew at first whose daughter she was
though someone pulled her skirt down for decency
the smell of alcohol and fuel everywhere
her lipstick so so red beneath the headlights
they couldn't take their eyes from her lips
what was she doing in a wild car like that? who was she?

at night I shivered in bed wondering how to get out of town
side-stepping wrecks they were everywhere on all the roads heading out toward the lights and laughter
a dented hubcap an amazing shoe with its laces still done up made you wonder how someone could step right out of a shoe like that like the flesh was willing or surprised or not there to begin with

in nightmares angry lords walked through my room
it took my breath away how ferocious love could be
sometimes jesus hung on the wall or was it the shadow of an elm?

in the morning at the kitchen table green tomatoes on the window
 sill we held devotions with careful hands
father's eyes focussed hard on me so he wouldn't remember but of
 course he did
listening often to mother's sunny childhood dreams
I thought I was free I was a child with a dancing mother
and my town was filled with children and my town had backstreets
 and sheds and black dogs and sugar trees but she disappeared
 and he died and I got out I'm getting out I'm getting out
what I left there the child gathering raspberries in an enamel bowl
he's not dead he went back to where you are before you're born
 again
waiting for the next time and another town

WEDDING MUSIC

mother took off her wedding ring
and laid it on the piano

she leaned sideways
to see if her foot was on the right pedal

she clenched and unclenched
her hands above the keyboard

then   as she swayed toward the music sheet
her fingers descended like snow

I saw the white skin on her finger
where her marriage had been

DREAM OF THE BLACK RIVER

I'm dreaming a dream of the black river where I can't swim I'm
    dreaming my last breath I'm dreaming how things are almost
    over I'm dreaming a possible swimmer with powerful arms to
    hold me
the river is cruel and cold I would drown for warmth
my legs dangle beneath me in the water my hands perform circles
    my lips are open for a kiss who will kiss them?

a figure on shore I can make it out someone knows I'm out
    here someone appears poised on a rock a diver about to
    thread evening air and enter this dark water
but no one moves there is only a pose of intention and nothing
    happens ever again

my darling lord take me all the way my fishtailing body my
    hearing my faithful tongue
show me early morning first light across yellow fields could
    crack my heart
I had eyes enough to see it all blue eyes that didn't care except
    to see and see and see
I stood in the long grass and turned around and around it was
    all there all the love its earth and flight and the rain at night
move me again my darling I used to unlace my shoes and go
    barefoot I walked through grass felt the earthworm's trembling
    tunnel sometimes I was so light I walked above ground it
    made me laugh my legs streaming with power or light I could
    see it shining in my veins I was a snake sloughing his life
    with no hope for another there was nothing to want or need
    or do there was nothing

nothing feels like something when you straddle a bough high in
    the sugar tree or ma's singing in the kitchen
when you love someone feels so light you could walk without
    shoes anywhere you could doff your hat and fly

my love take me away all the way to where my lies are true
take me beneath your umbrella of water that will be good enough
    for me to stand in the rain dreaming the dreams of the dead
    and living dogs barking in backyards remembering the love
    and terror that brought me here
my beauty lay me down and take me all the way I'm dreaming
    the dream of my death or someone is it doesn't feel like me
    anymore
he's gasping the river is in his ears he's banging at the window
    he wants to break into the swimmer's dream he wants another
    another

ANNA (FIRST DANCE)

we walk from streetlight to streetlight
silence to silence
how to speak about the human heart and memory
how to speak about all the rooms we live in

anna akhmatova wrote love poems before the russian revolution. everything changed. her former husband, gumilyev, also a poet, was executed for unspecified reasons in the early '20s. later, their young son was thrown into prison. primarily, it appears, to keep akhmatova silent.

during the '30s a few poems were put on paper, a few of those hand-copied and passed around. mostly akhmatova was silent. in her heart and mind she wrote poems but, for her child, she kept a public silence. these were the years of famine and purges and show trials. akhmatova, along with friends like the madelstams and pasternak, never knew when stalin would point at her.

after stalin's death, her poems began to appear in publications. strangers often stopped her on the street to thank her for the poems, not only for those few published but for the unwritten ones they knew she had lived. if it's possible for one woman's silence to save the soul of a nation, perhaps a world, this is what akhmatova did. she lived her people's silence, and their poems.

in the later '40s the commissar of culture, let him remain nameless, publicly denounced and ridiculed akhmatova as the "nun and whore" of russian literature. this referred to the fact that akhmatova wrote love poems of several kinds, that she lived and wrote equally in the spirit and the flesh.

akhmatova's silence of the '30s overlaps another kind of silence of the same time. alberto giacometti, who died in '66, the same year as akhmatova, was a swiss sculptor working in paris. for almost a decade he produced next to nothing. each sculpture disappeared. a few small figurines, small enough to fit into matchboxes, survived. giacometti kept sculpting, working toward what he saw, hammering, carving, chipping until there was nothing.

this was a silence. a silence of his materials, if not his process. through the rigours of this merciless vision his famous later sculptures emerged, elongated and thin, almost air. his work was not about objects. they almost disappeared. it was not about society. his work was about itself. his silence was about the act of seeing.

and akhmatova's silences were about being.

how to speak once more about the flesh and the spirit
the red heart and the blue wind

let's say it was 1958 *sail along silvery moon* was on the radio
it was sunday afternoon in july I remember the river and
swallows swooping low over the water
silver medallions fluttering on their chests the catholic boys
ran along the springboard and jack-knifed into the seine
river
there was something ominous about the muddy water like a
dream anything could be there venomous snakes weeds
and roots to clutch at you or simply depth something
ominous and those lean white bodies of faith disappearing
with graceful dives
I held my breath each time wondering if this one would
drown forever and not return how could he possibly rise
from that darkness of river and overhanging trees how
could the water give him back to light?
but always each boy exploded into air returning from death
or dreams flinging wet hair from his eyes shouting defiance
at the shore and each of us shivering there
and then the sun was so bright dancing in the spray around
the diver's head so bright on his long arms cleaving water
you could hardly believe in anything

let's say it was 1958 I was sitting on the fender of father's blue
dodge and it was sunday and I didn't want to ever leave the
river again

I was eating a persimmon trying to think of God it didn't
work my tongue wouldn't let me get away with it
there are no miracles only mirages in the desert and
disappearances in the river
there's nothing human that isn't betrayed and I know nothing
but what's human my hands my tongue and my face in a
mirror

grandmother wouldn't show me her photographs said I'd
never know what I couldn't would I? her life before me
but I think I remember her in the orchard she was a girl her
hair was soft and flowing down her back her legs brown
with sun
she said sometimes there were angels in the orchard she saw
them among the trees but she wasn't sure and if there were
what should she do?
sometimes there was a black dog or the neighbour's boy with
a stick sometimes there was nothing she could remember
and she was running for her life
this is how she learned to pray she said this is how she
worked her way out her hands at the clothes-line her eyes
on the sky

I don't love the prayer rug obedience or disobedience nothing
that absolute I love the babylonian body and the human
wound I love the surprising word the sinuous approach I
like the world approximately
the way grandfather smoked a cigarette in the garden his feet
lost among the potato plants the way he smiled and I
smelled the drifting smoke his stories hovering among the
raspberry canes the way he leaned on his hoe forever
I love words in the air balanced between mouths and ears I
love the way they're smoke before they're stone
but it's true I think there's not much a voice can say there's a
limit I guess to art there's no end to desire

stepping from shadow I shiver beneath a streetlamp there's
never enough light
I'm waiting for her she'll be wearing black I imagine her
undressing slowly my eyes are raw with looking

I imagine the beauty I see there are such possibilities in these
distances
I almost jump from my skin I want to reach out to what I
imagine

always knocking at the window maybe I'll find myself there
    each window a possible mirror
is this eros? longing for consummation in another place on
    another day?

I want to break the glass
I want to touch her everywhere

she knows I'm a left-eyed son
seeking an end to memory

she knows I'm an animal of temptations
that I speak out of desire
that I want to disappear at the hem of her flesh

she invites me to read her eyes
I see my hesitation there
on the porch as I reach to knock
and time and again step aside
just when light falls from the opening door

I recognize my pale defiance
I tell her it's all I have
that I don't want a way out
I want to walk in light
I don't want to be caught

she says that somewhere between yes and no
I can answer for myself

that I will end
how my kind ends
looking for other conversations
in other rooms

gregory told a story gregory's from kiev. there was a big fire, a fire so hot no one ventured within a hundred yards of it. barricades were thrown up and firemen tried to get enough pressure in their hoses to reach the distant flames.

the fire was raging out of control everything seemed lost until suddenly a firetruck sped down the street, smashed through the barriers and drove right into the heart of the burning building. a lone fireman leaped from the truck, grabbed a hose and flailed it in all directions. after ten or fifteen minutes the flames died down enough for the other firemen to move in closer and direct their nozzles onto the fire. it wasn't long before the fire was extinguished.

some weeks later a ceremony was held honouring the lone fireman who had courageously doused the inferno. the fire chief, and other dignitaries, praised him fulsomely, and they awarded him $5000. when he handed over the cheque, the chief asked what he would do with the money.

"well," he replied, "the first thing I will do is repair my brakes."

I love her hands the way they touch the garden
I love her hands in water the way they move there or when
    she is silent how they heal
I love how she gathers the world with her hands and lets it
    slip

something about all the rooms I have inhabited the way they
    held and released me
rooms that were cloisters or rooms with lamps and seashells
    and empty bottles
rooms with pianos or angels rooms where voices died rooms
    that were dance-halls for wallflowers

something about rooms the way a room could be a heart filled
with yearning the way the telephone suddenly rang and the
room opened to the world

I remember the night my daughter was born a storm broke all
the windows in the house when I returned home the wind
was blowing through the rooms

rooms of prayer or despair rooms of light

I was standing at the window someone was knocking I went
to the door but no one was there just children laughing
down the street

I was caught in the rain it was the day I knew my death not
everyone's that lucky
everything came together everything was there my footsteps
behind my footsteps ahead my unborn children everything
was there and I knew the number of my days but I lost it
my bones are white it's what I know from grandfather's farm
what's left in the fall scattered bones where horses wheeled
all summer the wind low in the grass and the sudden cold
sweeping rain
I lost everything I thought I was and had didn't have a thing
it was a lie I made didn't know I was that kind of god
didn't know I'd believe my own memory

sometimes it feels like I'm sculpted don't know anymore
who's sculptor who's shaped
like giacometti's figurines not carved from but toward
something I'm sculpted into dust until there's nothing there
or something like nothing
I must think this is some version of divinity what else to call it
there's no purpose here there's nothing to know there's just
this seeing this continual seeing

I must think this is leading somewhere that I am at that
    random moment when the chisel can't stop and chips a last
    feature into crumbs when I'm plaster dust in the sculptor's
    hair or his white footprints on the street

something about the river I heard ice grind in my sleep
something about rivers how they touch what we forget
there's no end to the river where we walk there's no end to
    our walk

it doesn't take much a scent of lilacs or rose oil a song it
    doesn't take much to remember the world always how it
    was the way memory spills through what I see or touch or
    hear and there's no end to it like desire

I remember there was no need for the altar icons or text I
    didn't know I was being tried
I was barefoot for a moment like grandmother before me
    looking for my shoes something to make me human I was
    looking for a hat not just any hat my hat I was looking for a hat

memory is a scar I love to touch but will never trust
the future because I was born I trust and can never touch
so I straddle time taking the scraps memory offers and wanting
    them again and again

grandmother at the clothes-line the sculptor's baffled hands
    grandfather leaning on his hoe
this is what I know until the end of memory

I walk with her she holds her umbrella above us like a petal
    like ribs holding a heart like the opening cage of the sky
we throw stones into the river we jump pools of water the
    moon's beneath our feet

I was eating a persimmon there's not much to believe or say
    there are mirages in the mirror yes I betray my tongue with
    silence I'm shivering with delight

Kristjana Gunnars

FROM MEMORY V

leave quebec late at night
for montreal, 180 miles southwest
gulls & hawks circle
in the distancing east

the legs of the young ones
soft, pulpy with water
have to be opened to dry
the scales drop quickly, quickly

pelicans stand on stumps
at the shrinking pier, a heavy
vulture lands on a wagging branch

have to slit it down the length
of its back, under the toes
down to the last joint, have to
remove the tendons

have to write a daybook

arrive montreal midday
tuesday august 1, eat
the daymeal, walk in the brush
gather quills for a daybook

quills of young ducks, geese
still in the pin-feather age
quills full of water, blood
slow-drying, fly-blown

soft, have to slit them
soak the liquid up on paper
have to paint them outside
turn the pages heavy with them

have to write a daybook
with moist scaly quills
write a book of settlements
on the way to kingston

slow-drying, fly-blown

JÓHANN BRIEM II

the steamship verona reaches
granton on thursday july 6
& heads straight to glascow

we've begun to rehearse how
to see in darkness, to see
that which is hidden, to win
the love of strangers, to understand

the speech of birds, the foreign
tongues

on tuesday july 11 the allanline's
austria leaves for quebec

we've left our books in múlasýsla
to be burned, this will be
from memory, even bólu-einar
andrésson's books were burned

in 1885, there are over 700
of us to learn the methods
from memory: how to see

by night; smear the blood
of a mouse, the belly of a white
rabbit, the eyeball of an eagle
around your eyes: how to see

hidden things; how to succeed;
dry a raven's head in the wind
where no sun shines & a white
black stone drops from the brain

wind the stone in unused flax
& carry it under your left armpit:
how to win love; dry
a pigeon's heart & hang it

round your neck, all will love you

JÓHANN BRIEM IV

the finest wizard of the north

saemundur fródi says
there are other ways
to escape a sense of evil
on a wicked journey

by steamship north
on red river august 5
two large flatboats like eyes
one tied on each side
of the steamer, looking east
looking west, arriving

in winnipeg tuesday august 8
six o clock at night

where a human brain is buried
in thought of winter
& memory is three months long
towards the north

to flee the man
who doesn't want you, don't
recite the our
father forwards & backwards

saemundur fródi says
there are other ways
soak a stolen brass
in your own blood

pull an eye
pull a man's head
out of your own blood

steal an imp
of a man's rib
from a grave at whitsun

galdra-leifi, another wizard
watered a man's head
with wine & bread
& with it he read the future

what they'll pull from your blood
once you're dead

but death isn't necessary
saemundur fródi says

there are other ways

to journey the north

STEFÁN EYJÓLFSSON XIV

i'm down to collecting skeletons
bones with deeper relations
than flesh or skin, bones that show
how we live, seven

are dead at fridjón's, two
left, at ólafur's the third
baby swells in the gums
blood streaks the white teeth

scurvy cuts away the flesh
as cleanly as it can, removes
the skin, viscera, bones
too small, too delicate

to be touched hang together
by thin ligaments, tags
of leather separate the segments
the hatchets of disease do

rough work among us
cut the tendons that join
cheek bones, pelvic bones, deep
bones loosen like ribs

i'm buckling under, can't watch
ólafur's third one bruise, swell
thirty five are dead, every
third one of us, a child

a weak adult, the saw
of scurvy picks away
the eyes, scrapes the brain
out of the skull, washes out

the loosened brain, folds
the legs, limbs, ties up
the marrowed bones in rags
bones, deep bleeding bones, see

how we hang in the sun to dry

THORLEIFUR JÓAKIMSSON, DAYBOOK II

august 21, 1876: (heard it
said, survive in the great
plains, survive anywhere)

only just beginning to

learn grasshopper hunting
since april 20, mild

small rain all summer
today is the first large
grasshopper harvest, all

summer at daybreak
picked them off the tops
of tall grass stalks, one

by one, cold, unmoving
in the nightchill, folded wings
mouth-sucking, rubbing

for song: the edge
of a wing across ribs, hind
legs (heard it said

they multiply in big
groups, migrate vast
distances, destroy large

fields, crops) today
prepared a row of dry
grass, a willow broom, swept

the herd sprinkling
into flames in the grass
small rain of insects, charred

in dawn, harvested scorched

today is the first step
on black stubble, warm
after the cold nightspell

i'm only just beginning

DEAD

my fathers are dead
buried in scars
under the winter road
the horse we shared
is all that's left

still sturdy
the road still long
weaves between black hills
over an underworld
easily recalled

the farmgates with mad dogs
easily passed
as the story of hermódur
in the eddas he rides
to find a medium, crosses
a bridge over clefts
asks how to recall
his brother baldur

more easily recalled
than it appears
rivers flash-flood in spring
once they start

but i prefer dead winter
dry as triesnecker, small
scarred crater in the west
great as tiny hyginus
linked with valleys
ridges with ariadaeus, another

name of no recall

unlike the dead fathers
easily recalled, dead
as in the first years
we ride through valleys
& look for small signs
of spring

SLAUGHTERHOUSE 2

white sheepskins punch
like clockwork out
of a cleft in the wall
a pile of bloodied fleece
swells into mountain

the finished product
i can stand, but inside
there is flaying
heads are lopped off
water trickles down walls
like cave linings
that i don't want to know

the lonely head
that speaks a whole story

how one-eye lost the other
eye, you see
the vanir decapitated mímir
preserved his head with herbs
chanted it with spells
& it worked, one-eye
asked about time
& it answered back

you see, spring burst
from mímir's open neck
under the yggdrasill tree
& one-eye gave the other eye
to see
the mirror as crystal sphere
to drink water of prophesy

this i don't want to enter
further
lumps swell, we name them
& don't stand on them

plains of sosigenes (named
after an astronomer
who changed the calendar)
plateaus of plinius, mountains
named apennines, haemus, hadley

this i only want to see
with one eye
through a two-inch telescope
blotches, from afar

BLIND 2

the end begins
with profuse rain
when all on earth weeps
into puddles, street sloughs
on such a night
reykavík falls ugly

it's true, the mother frigg
asks for this weeping
pouring of tears

to make water flow
in the cracks of crater flamstead
to fill the oceanus procellarum
the dominant dry sea
to rush down the carpathian
mountains between copernicus
& cape bernat on moon

that's the place
that concerns me now
the still dry face
that won't weep

the end begins this way
baldur packed & burned
with his ship, horse, wife
as if to sail, ride, beget
children over there
in the cracked mountainring
around flamstead, it's true
one-eye gave draupnir
to recall

a useless old story
slashing through torrents
windy night of my city
deep inside, my reykavík
falls
ugly

into the one-eyed dream
i can't get out of

CHANGELING XVII

this is the end

now i recognize them
tove, gunnar, sister gunna by name
eleven hundred years of family
they're used to me too

& they want me away again
like they want to get rid of lice
but it's too late
i'm rooted in rock
remember, you put me there

no live cat bound to your back overnight
no patch of cathide tied to your shoulders
no streaking round the farm naked
once, twice, three times in hailstorm
will bring the tumour of my name out
onto your skin
where you can puncture me like a boil
like an uncalled-for growth

what begins deep in thighs
can't be gotten rid of
i'm here to stay, to remember

MONKSHOOD XXVIII

close my eyes
i'll try to escape through my eyes if you don't
find myself again
embroidering this way quietly with girls

sewing cartwheels on a spectacle case

blind me to the shadow of what's to be
the damp meadows behind the wheatfields
slipping away with the cartwheel mender
threading through clumps of poison parsley

clawing with arms & legs
needling night into the kecksies

unseen, faceless shadows
lying among the blotched stems

hemlock leaves drop on my eyes
an unfamiliar hand strokes my brow
in an unknown country
a mother i never knew responds
with words i never heard

blind me to the corobanes
the spider that slips down
into the needlework of fine hair
the purple body that struggles
deep, under

the white-laced hemlock net
quietly like this
a slow patch of black spreads
in the damp blotting-paper sky

WAKEPICK I

tonight i disentangle
soft underwool fibre from coarse hairs
make ready for carding

rain blasts at the membrane window
the mud walls are damp
begin to leak, little by little
onto the sleeping benches

i escape this flood in the work of hands
pretend not to see the paste
of whiteflies trod underfoot
into the soft mud floor
pretend not to feel clammy & cold

we have no use for human fleas
no use for bland horsehair & wool

tonight again i pretend
to be salt
i separate myself again
fine from coarse
die another death tonight

& when i'm dead
i turn to knotweed on the knolls
to starlings in the rain
i turn blood, hair, bone
i turn to stone

in the work of my hands
i turn my fragments up from the floor
blood & bone from the floor
make ready for another rain
tonight again

i disentangle sinew, hair
i turn to stone

STRAW HIVE

honey boxes
with rain-shedding roofs, slanting
and clean straw packed in tight
bound with wire:

the bees were glad of the straw
cool in summer
warm in winter
they buzz under the house-apiary still
though the hive is gone

like winter
smoothed in the brome of time
the fields once kept bright red and blue
and dark green now
ribbed and veined with brome

the storm gathers dust
and i see you clearly in the brown distance
you too have been shed by time

but i was grateful for you then

the clean desire
to be bound in the wires of your arms
and the memory fades
the buzz of bees dies out

but i can watch them go forever

DWARF PEAR

there were trees budded
kept small
short-lived: unprofitable, they said
unworthy

they were garden dwarf trees
high-culture trees
made with hours of judicious pruning

i remember fathers gathering
the easy flourish of many years
loaded with fruit
a year from the bud

fathers who argued the incessant success

i lie in the manna grass again
remember those tall sayings
and how easily my thoughts rupture
how fast you flow out

the sloughs of loss:
was our culture then not coarse enough—
how miniature we kept our love
how we erased the wet meadows

and when the dwarf threatened to bear fruit
we thought of death, no
we thought of murder
we thought of keeping the small small love
unworthy

AFTER SHEARING WE WASHED

after shearing we washed
the wool in old urine and water
dried in sun, rinsed

in straw baskets in the stream
the washing pot at the riverside
on glowing coals, we stirred

the tangles with a stick
poured them on a raft
floating above the falls

spread out on the grass
the day's work over
there were wild vegetables

goosefoot and sea kale
in flowering bud, we had
tenderness to cultivate

bitterness to blanch
the tang of strong washes
the texture of sun-dried wool

turned into dream
the growth of a garden
we have removed from the body

bleached in the river
that falls across years
and dissipates into sea

THE NIGHT REFUSES TO BE COLD

the night refuses to be cold
deprives me of preparations
steals in on the afternoon
too gentle to be noticed

time passes without my knowing
I watch the numbers on the clock
slip by without effort

time is where you are
your silent steps down the stairs
your silent breath when you sleep
your imperceptible touch

when you are not you
but I in another form
a shadow of what is forgotten
when your face is my face

looking back at me
trying to say with your eyes
what that time was like

when I really was you
and you were the air I breathed
dark and indistinct
you were the night in me

in winter there are no colours
no gossamer webs
in the grass in the dew

only barren branches above the fence
and crusty brown leaves that refuse to let go

only the silence of spreading frost

THE MILD WINTER MORNING

the mild winter morning
when birds have ventured out to sound
against the grey sky
knowing their tiny voices
will not hurry the sun

knowing my poem will not move
snow to melt or grass to sprout
nonetheless I write

incompetent against the great clouds
my poem a form of breathing
a form of longing
to say over the frozen snow

that I think of you
without thought
that your image like a dream
recedes when sought
that the memory of spring is old
and of another world

MY PARENTS, ATTEMPTING

my parents, attempting to take over the work of God, bought a sunlamp so it could shine on me. so began the hours of darkness that filled my childhood. it was a strict routine I was honour bound to follow in order to be normal again. every day the door was closed and I was left in a dark room, naked before the glow of the lamp. it was an ominous metallic light that made the room smell like the burning of limestone and I knew it was dangerous. I knew it was somehow a replica of life to react to danger by taking the clothes off and lying down beside it.

I THINK THE WIND IS BETWEEN US

I think the wind is between us

I know the wind gushes
over miles of cold prairie
where nothing else is
but ground and sky

all that emptiness between us
that reminds me of what passes
lives we have lived

in the light of my only lamp
the past vanishes like darkness
and I can see in this present
you are not here

you are not within hearing
and the windows rattle in the storm

John V. Hicks

KEEP QUITE STILL

Puff and drift from those far chimneys
where old-fashioned men with shovels
bank their fires

will reach you if you
keep quite still
if you

let tendrils of air
find one nostril and another
and what they bring

offering and gift of memory
form in the blood
to recitations of the ticking clock

coal smoke releasing fragrance
of long ago forests
whose birds spread their songs like wings

listen

keep quite
still

CAROL IN THREE-THREE TIME

The woman with ice-blue eyes
sweeps my floor clean of song sheets
and sonnet forms addressed to
my true love my true love;
(What have I done for my—true love?)
has laid table for two with clean linen
woven of discarded counterpoints;
(What have I done?)
                                        the kettle
fills the hearth's cavern with snatches
of twelve-tone scale;

                                        line and space,
minims have trimmed their stems
half way to my rhythms,
(This have I done for my—true love)
crotchets quaver in confrontations
with slanted bar lines,

and the singers will frown and falter
fumble-tongue through traditional phrases;
the singers will crumple scripts and hurry
back to their vocalises,
cringe at the rule of three
invading their practice sessions,
thumb frantic through lexicons
of musical notation;
                                        accompanists
required for last minute rehearsals
will not answer their telephones;

and who will be here to inaugurate
the vernal ceremonies
the thrust through wet black earth
of hyacinth and tulip blade
who
but the woman with ice-blue eyes
my true love my true love?

READING ROOM

Largely as I suppose to neutral-
ize intimidations of children,
a big fat purple snake, erectus, dominates
one wall. Saucer eyes
stare not unkindly over the low tables;
tongue at full flick
suggests a moistening of lips pre-
paratory to the making of apology.

Old sinmonger, I could say, creator
of great originals, you do well to take
the sacrament of innocence to your com-
fort; to tune vibrations of the deaf ear
with whispers of the morning music
of children laughing unashamedly
on street corners, calling encouragements
into unsavoury dark alleys.

DARK MORNING

Mother, there's a pterodactyl
perched on our aerial. He
bends it. When he folded his wings
he made the sun come out.

    Omens of extinction are
    everywhere. We don't need
    visitations of forgotten reptiles
    to twist our antennae awry.

You thought it was a dark morning.
It was his wing span, I tell you—
how many inches? No—pterodactyls
don't answer to inches.

    Hand me that duster, will you?
    Every day is a dark morning.

Here, mother. Let's not go extinct.
He's sitting there inventing feathers.

THE TALK OF THE TOWN

Yes you were indeed; sidewalk sparrows,
seldom out of chatter, included you
gladly; smiling panes,
bright with your reflection, provoked song
on the lips of the cleaners
any mint morning.

They were no simple amenities
small groups on corners
bandied like bells; they were
your name and your splendour,
the chime of your every passing
that soared above traffic, lighted
on staff and pennant stem,
held noon's or night's zenith ablaze.

Small wonder when you plunged
down that horizon, dragging sunset with you,
the hundred normalities returned
one by one to their accustomed places,
streets settled back
to dull traffic sounds, dust, soiled windows.

DO NOT DISTURB

I shall come out when I am ready.
This I implore:
do not speak,
do not so much as breathe at my door
one syllable, nor break
for an instant the stupor her heady
and drugged vintage induces.
Let none enter; if necessary annoy
my friends; meet my enemies, sign truces;
let me alone, balanced on this razor's edge of joy.
I shall come out and begin sorrow over
in due time, in the mercy of this lover.

RUBBER BOOT BOY

Rubber boot boy, I can't come out to play,
no, not today,
the world being mud and streaming wet;
not, not yet.
Here, fed and warm,
I shall take little harm.
Food, firelight and indolence
make indeed middling sense
to misadventurers whose
conditionings elect to choose
pine crackle and kettle steam
to accompany a theme,
rubber boot boy,
for solitary thoughts' employ;
thoughts, I grant, that will a moment stray
watching you squelch away.

NIGHT FLIGHT

Flitmouse, somewhile after sunset,
blinking, unhooked himself from where he hung,
spread as it were twin snippets from a skin umbrella,
and mounted the ladder of darkness rung by rung.

Of instant veer, of dip and flutter,
his knowledge being a quiet exhaustive thing,
he nonchalantly employed such aerobatics as would
have put to shame the fleetest feather a-wing.

He, the embodiment of silence,
shadow to shadow sped a lonely flight;
what comforts lay in her arms folded about him
were secrets kept between himself and night.

URSA MAJOR
(after Basque myths)

Argument

Two thieves purloin from farm
a brace of oxen. Farmer sends
servant in pursuit. Servant
does not come back. Sends housekeeper
accompanied by dog. Neither
return. Raging in anger,
takes the trail himself. For temper's sake
condemned to roam the sky forever
There they are, season by season,
tail up, tail down, acting out
their story on the zodiac stage
to the ever changing audience of the earth.

Dubhe, Merak (the oxen)

Dull beasts, could you not know
you were being rustled? Nor recognize
thievish command, the unfamiliar goad,
the stealthy movement, being urged
out of the stall by subtlety, the march
splayfoot into the night? Innocence
falsified? Could the slow brain
not guess it was deceit
that turned the comfort of the byre
into the chill air, the darkness
where no plough turned? Your stubborn bulk
had thwarted them; none could move you
against your brute wills. The chance to stand
upon your rights is lost forever now.
So it is with the too easily led;
strengths melt where the spirit fails.

Megrez, Phecda (the thieves)

To take your prey was simple, will
so easily bent scarcely a distinction
in the approved techniques of
the criminal mind. Had you essayed
the feathered brood and all its instant
reactions, a fright of squawkings
alerting alike management and staff
to what you were up to; that would have been
a chapter in crime's annals
worthy of general circulation.
Anyway, you did it; the submissive hulks,
trained in slow responses, moved
to your purpose. Elementary as it was,
it did its damage; it laid plot
to one more convolution of the mind
seeking reason out of chaos. Tales
conceived on a slow journey can explain
even the movements of companion worlds.

Alioth (the servant)

It was not in your contract; you
could easily have drawn this fact,
respectfully, to the consideration
of an employer. There were no unions
to interpose bargaining between
master and minion, to lay down
letter-for-letter terms. The merit of
direct discussion is apparent
now, movement of the mindless mass
having worked out function to a point
where we can spot the niceties
of error. Well, you went
where you were bidden, not questioning

command. We ascribe still
nobility even to suicidal missions
in honour of obedience. Consider this
your heavenly memorial. It sounds better
than a sneer, a snort of dismissal.

Mizar (the housekeeper)

Little doubt you were better at supervision
of cleaning, of serving meals, recording
expenses, attending to purchases
of adequate provisions, making sure
appliances were in working order,
than undertaking missions of enquiry,
particularly this one, following the trail
of a lost servant, dependent upon
a playful canine snout, itself untrained
in tracking. A little argument, an
appeal to reason, might have kept you
at your post. Perhaps you were too eager
for a change of air, a break from
details of your tedious occupation.
You did no good; your double venture
is a bent handle now, engraved
for all to see, an enjoinder to let
well enough alone, not to take on
tasks for which one stands
ill equipped, that point to a lost way.

Alcor (the dog)

Little dog, where are you trotting?
Does the servant's scent
not tell you something's wrong tonight,
that here was no foray to the fields
to turn the loam for planting? Think;

you should have clamoured at the master's door,
rousing the household, yapping
alarums. Thievery abroad
and you all unconcerned? For shame.
The watchdog fails in duty, evil intent
unthwarted. Stars unnumbered
testify against you. Sleeping sentries
do not die in bed. You had better stay
on the trail you follow.

Alkaid (the farmer)

The whole thing is visionary. Are you sure
you didn't dream it? Too late now
ever to sort truth from the deceptions
of the fertile mind. You are too far
ever to hail, ever to be expected
to flash back answers. Time prints you
on its dark curtain, and we are left
with our surmisals. If it be true,
it was a harsh way of teaching
the lesson of the lost temper. We,
aware of tempers and the dire handout
of sentences to invoke destruction,
go headstrong as you went, too obstinate
to swerve from purpose of revenge
and get us back on course. Perhaps
history, indifferent, so repeats us all
that our small conflicts are
the echoes of a sounding brass
now and again in circuits
about the binding of the magnet pole.
Go on forever, staff, cattle, thieves
too far dispersed ever to find trace,
though from timeless distance we may keep
an indifferent eye upon the lot of you.

Q.E.D.

The problem is to put silence into speech
without breaking it; to leave
on water the image of the face peering
over the stern; to cause to feel
textures in the air like leaves,
in the air itself, shapeless, not
visible as poeticizing a season,
but, sensible to the undrawn breath,
becoming in form an approximation
of imprint.
                    What succeeds
presents itself a waiting candidate
to be acknowledged, recorded,
and in proper sequence summoned for
interview; another problem.
The rationale of its movement
must become what was to be proved,
attract tone formations
proving what it was to become.

FROG ON A LEASH

Rhythmic tugging at finger ends
parallels signals of impalement
the angler knows. Live food
is a false offering, a garnish
piqued with death.
                    The walk is
beyond environment. One plunge
would break sequences, let sink into
appropriate depths and up again
sunned and glistening.

An unnatural
attachment. This sweep of earth
eschews traversing in little
leaps and bounds. The tug is
continually at the heart, applies
innumerable small distresses. I
measure vainly the halting step
on this jumpy journey.

FULL MOON

That that smudged wafer up there,
perfect one night only, should inspire
blood rage in the lovers, quickening
of pulses toward the life surge,
were paradox enough. Could they not have chosen
spouting peak or lava stream
or the upthrust of forest trunk to engender
their apostrophes and praises?

Were they not told the thing is dead?

No need to cite for further comment
its others in subjection, the stricken brain,
tongue given to insensate argument,
legally irresponsible, beyond reproach.

A dead world for lovers, madmen?

Yet sail, pale disc with dirty face,
on your errands. Present yourself as symbol
of peace, quiet, unknown to both. Your
message, calm always in the reading, tells
that death at last marches to victory, that
we too, in its throes, may go rejoicing.

YOU KNOW I CANNOT COME

You know I cannot come to your castle room;
someone would hear faint grindings of machinery
and come running
and find us clinging to the stone cold wall.

You know I cannot come to your warm darknesses;
someone would hear wave upon wave of sighing
and peal alarums
and learn too late the song issues without sound.

You know I cannot come to your interring;
someone would see two shadows twining among tree shapes
and bring books
and expunge *Rest, Peace,* from the false waiting stone.

Air we breathe is our own sweet undoing;
water betrays us, we are lost daily everywhere;
and sunly about you spring
flowers on paths down which you know I cannot come.

Robert Kroetsch

THE SILENT POET SEQUENCE

The Silent Poet Sees Red

and green too, on occasion, granted
but I wouldn't slander a friend for the world, cross
my heart
and spit to die
but he shuts off his inboard motor, he sprawls on the
deck of his cottage, nursing a beer, he forgets to
shave for a week
and he thinks he's a sailor, Earache the Red; it was he
who discovered dry land
but sit yourself down, he promises, life is short
and while you're up, crack us a couple of cold ones,
poet
but I hardly have time, he talks too much; he is Professor
of Nowhere at some place or other; puck, he says,
waving a stick
and he skates his way through class, defying entropy,
slamming the puck under the chairs of his sleeping
students
but women are fooled by his library, ha; he's all show;
may he rupture himself, clipping his toenails
and while I'm on the subject, his wife has four arms,
she holds him together, blind as love
but remember, the pupil is black, we see with darkness
only

and I watch for a light in the west, occidents will
happen, ho
but sunrise comes at noon to her bed
and what do we have for lunch, breakfast; Silent Poet,
she tells me, you are the great keeper, the wellspring
of was, the guardian of ought
but that's your loss, not mine
and soft as blue she whispers a pip into her palm; west
is the colour of the wind

The Silent Poet Moves His Office

but I can't throw this away
and the Maalox, god knows I'll need that; some lead for
a pencil, ha, well
but the keys; okay, so what if a door does come knocking
and this paper knife, tarnished almost black, Watzernaym
left it, open the mail, she said, I send you
but she must have forgot
and the English penny that didn't bring luck
but Earache the Red appears in my doorway, gives me the
willies; ho, he says, caught you
and I'm guilty, I blush; surreptitiously I check my
fly; saw the boxes out in the hall
but what, he adds, exactly, is the function of objects,
if you don't mind my asking
and he answers, waving a book, this yours by any chance
but I'm holding a packet of papers, the band breaks,
the rubber is old
and I pick up a letter, from a patient in the asylum;
you love me, she says, I can tell by your poems; the
broken draft of her address, there in the corner; I

was going to scrawl her a note, a quick apology
even, maybe send her something
but I open the Maalox
and Earache the Red is shouting, the blur in his hand a
mousetrap, the blood confused me, in the wire frame,
the staring eyes; we transfer memory, he
predicates; more easily put, we chicken
but I take the book, words that I've never seen before,
underlined by my assertion
and Earache the Red is raving, the object is, he says,
not to object, get it; he peeks out into the hall;
he farts
but consider, picking up three sticks of chalk; he
points; consider this ruler you've carried with
you, from boyhood on; this embarrassing print of
a rapids you never hang, this tape you haven't the
courage to hear; consider, my friend; he points;
this homemade valentine, this pair of scissors,
this rock
and I think to myself, I'm sorry, forgive me, I didn't
mean it
but I go down the hall, my wrists in pain, carrying
everything

The Silent Poet at Intermission

but who are all these strangers, I ask
and I mean it, heading for the bar
but trust my luck, Earache the Red, a drink in either
hand, announces, Madame Sosostris has a bad cold this
evening, we laugh
and I say, that's pharaoh enough
but nobody gets it, I buy my own

and Earache, the crowd gathering, art should instruct,
he tells us, glancing at his own reflection
but not by painting the rainbow black, we laugh
and I have a pot myself, Labatt's did that much for me
but she who loves gold loves elsewhere
and follows the path prophesying no end, it's hardly hard
to guess; uppie uppie, she says in the morning, the
medium well done
but he hands her a glass, she looks; here's mud in your
eye
and even the Virgin Queen, she wasn't Shakespeare either
but I did scorn them all, she wrote
and with good cause: a leman is a lemon, ha; well, let the
heads fall
but music, he says, is the mothering lode; he waves his
arms; he is composing a series of dichotomies for
violin
and fiddle, the chiselling clod
but he spills his drink
and I wipe my shoe on my cuff; I hear the weasel that sniffs
the hen, the blood-loud blood in the gutter, the wise
man strangling on his own; sorry, mum
but he discovers, just then, the split of mind
and body; putting Descartes before the hearse, we laugh
but just as I raise the dagger the buzzer sounds, I am
left with the thought in my hand
and he takes her elbow in his palm; the news, he tells us,
straight to our backs, must learn to be old, to learn
to be new; we scratch ourselves
but follow, as we lead, to the first usher
and I leave for home, bumping knees with a dozen strangers
but never go

The Silent Poet Finds Out

and they'll get me, I know, dread or alive
but I go out at night, with my shovel, I dig deep holes
in the neighbours' lawns
and Earache the Red, at coffee, for god's sake hit the
sack early, he says, you look like you never sleep
but watch those dirty dreams; he winks
and shakes his spoon in my direction
but I don't let on that I understand
and the mayor is offering a reward, some maniac, he claims,
dug a toilet pit, directly in front of City Hall; the
reward is an insult, I'm worth more
but I look at the posters, I'm tempted, poets are not well
paid, I could use the money
and the grave in the bishop's garden, I don't think that was
mine, I never dig graves
but isn't that the truth, they see what they believe, people,
I go out at night, I dig deep holes
and a friend, late for a meeting, fell headlong into a gap
in the campus green
but didn't smile
and I was alone again in the world
but Earache, there's a new law, he says, you're legally
responsible for all your dreams
and I buy his coffee
but just last night, while he snored in her arms, I pitched
black dirt at his window
and walled him in
but he doesn't let on; he calls for a refill; I'm sweating
and he looks at the morning paper, then looks at me; in
China they've picked up a signal, I wait
but he takes three sugars, I hate that about him; quick
energy, he says; he winks
and I hide my blisters under the table

The Silent Poet Craves Immortality

and even black has its lighter moments, ha
but the doggerel of the sun is such, we stare blankly
and I stop criticizing my friends, I praise their ugly
 faces, their staggering poems
but they agree
and then I wonder at my own judgement; I nod; they slap
 my back, you've mellowed
but that makes it worse, I watch TV
and memorize the weather, promising, first thing in the
 morning, I'll write the last line
but secretly at night I turn signs around, I point
 all travellers in the wrong direction; I've so far
 derailed three trains; I look at bridges malignantly
and pray with the first two fingers of each hand crossed
but she, in the bathroom, washing between her legs, what
 are you doing on your knees
and I leap up
but I think I'm preparing to die, I can smell food inside
 a closed fridge, the milk a little sour, the onions
 gone soft, as in a wet garden, the hamburger practising
 green
and I bought new dishes yesterday, bright plates, Italian,
 flowers on a white background, six Japanese bowls, I
 can taste the roses
but cheap, something you could stack in a tomb, send out
 on the water
and Jezebel, she sees I'm reading in bed, I study maps,
 this is Alberta, I look for rivers that trail off into
 dotted lines, this is the Yucatan, this the Siberian
 forest; I peruse a linguistic atlas, looking for one word
but she knows I'm watching; she lifts a foot into the
 basin, slow as sin

and I put in a bid for a ship, a rust-eaten tanker, nothing
pretentious
but something, nevertheless, that will burn with a flare, ho
and give a signature to the sky

The Silent Poet Eats His Words

but whatever you do, don't
and remember, forget what I said about Watzernaym, miss or
hit, she didn't love me
but not in the way I wanted not to be loved, I've had enough
and that's only a start, she was an admirer of bricks, she
liked their fired faces, their false
but predictable ends
and darkness itself she would nothing
but praise, it falls, she said, not like you, feigning a
light
and I learned to hate from her loving, her ink pot, calling
the letter back; I teased her awake
but touch your typewriter, poet, she whispered, then I can
sleep in the morning
and that was a hard one to swallow, ho; I tried for an hour
but life is a series, I explained, I drew diagrams on the
frosted window, I brushed the wrinkles from the sheet
where I wanted her to lie
and after another failure I stood, delicately, on my own
head, defying her to tell up from down; love, I said,
I'm inclined to agree
but the penny saved is, generally, lost; a stitch in time
seams nothing, ha
and I argued, at length, for the inevitable rise of the
real, into Idea; this time it's forever, I added
but all my blood sank to my brain, I was left hanging, my
neck hurt; I was trying to amuse

and Ahab, I said, was a fool to marry you, Jezebel
but don't feel bad, I'm depressed myself, there's a flock
of two thousand birds that shits on my car, they sit
in this saskatoon bush, see, waiting
and when I drive up the leader says, shit
but sometimes I fool them; I hesitate; just as I open the
door
and after they've all obeyed the command, like the stooges
they are, I step out, regally, majestically, I step from
the car, I bow, just slightly; Francis, I say, is the
name; skip the saint business
but she was sound asleep, except for a rhythmic snoring,
suggesting she might be awake; please, she said, jerking
the covers from the place where I might have been, read
the review of your book again, make some coffee, scrub
that goddamn kitchen floor, vacuum, take your pulse,
fix the toaster, go put on your snow tires, asshole,
it's January

MILE ZERO

> " . . . hockey is a *transition game:* offence to defence, defence to offence, one team to another. Hundreds of tiny fragments of action, some leading somewhere, most going nowhere. Only one thing is clear. Grand designs don't work."
>
> -Ken Dryden, *The Game*

: being some account of a journey through
western Canada in the dead of six nights

1

I looked at the dust
on the police car hood.
I looked around the horizon.
(Insert here passage on
nature—

try: The sun was blight
enough for the wild rose.
A musky flavour on the milk
foretold the cracked earth . . .

try: One crow foresaw my fright,
leaned out of the scalding
air, and ate a grasshopper's
warning . . .

try; A whirlwind of gulls
burned the black field white,
burned white the dark ploughman
and the coming night . . .)

←————————————

I AM A SIMPLE POET
I wrote in the dust
on the police car hood.

Chateau (A Landing) Frontenac

crisp, and the wind
the winter bleat

rain and the best
are never mulled

champlain
is green

madonna
the river is hungry

champlain, look in
my window, wait

absurd as undertow
or word

the hurt of lovers
hand in hand

repay the rot
the risk, the rain

madonna
madrona

announce and
enter, adding (end)

champlain is green
has empty eyes

westering is
madrona, west

the wooden shore
to look inland

2

Where did the virgin come from
on my second night west?

> Let me, prosaically, parenthetically, remark
> from what I observed: the lady in question took
> from the left (or was it right?) pocket of her
> coffee-stained apron a small square pad of lined
> sheets of paper. She bit the wood back from
> the lead of a stub of pencil. And she wrote,
>
> without once stopping to think, the loveliest
> goddamned (I had gauged her breasts when she
> wiped the table) poem that Christ ever read.

She had a clean mind.

Driving, Accidental, West

1

the shaped infinity
to hammer home

help, and the wild geese
heading south

and every way and
which, confuse

the fall of light
the fatal peen

how, and the commonest
crow or sparrow

speak the pale
or sensing moon

2

accelerate, the swan
sing, or eloquent as

antelope, the crisp
rejoinder of the duck's

quack to the deer's
leap, and, even then

even, a static dream
twitter and acquit

the kill, wait, for
and the nasty snow

fall, fall and for
tonight, only, dream

3

On the third night west
a mountain stopped us.
The mountains were lined up
to dance. I raised my baton:
rooted in earth, the lightning
rod on the roof of the barn,
on my soul's body. A crow
flew over the moon. I raised
my baton, a moon, a mountain.
*

The crow flew over the mountain

---

*I have removed from this stanza the two lines

Verily, I insist: I did
not raise the purple crow

(and I like the ambiguity created by the line break)

partly because the "Verily" intrudes what we might call another language code, and that an unfortunate one in this case, for all the play on *truth*;

partly because the sexual innuendo puts me, as actual poet behind the implied speaker ("I") in a bad light; that is, self-mockery is, so to speak, harder to come by, as one (the poet, the implied speaker, the I or the "I") grows older (RK).

Descent, as Usual, into Hell

i've told her now so long
so often and sojourn *salut*

diamond
star or

(*ouest*
or quest or)

worry bead
relinquish

redolent as always
as the heated rose

summer and
a scent

(allot illusions as
is necessary to)

annealing praise
reticulate as tongue

mighty and a mouse
alike a maze

can he her up haul
or over if and may

asylum for her worship
in the night announce

the word of way
widen and weave

the was or is of
story is a story of

4

* Order, gentlemen. Order

is the ultimate ←
mountain. I raised my baton.

---

*I have removed from this stanza the single line

(her breasts were paradigms)

(originally in parenthesis, as indicated) because I am somewhat offended by the offhand reference to paradigm. And yet, is not the mother figure the figure at once most present in and most absent from this poet's work? The concern with *nostos* is related to a long family history of losses: *e.g.*, the paternal side of the family landing in New York in June, 1841, aboard the *Pauline*, and the mother of the large Kroetsch family, settled in Waterloo County, Ontario, a few years thereafter widowed, the early death of the poet's mother in Alberta, a century after that first un-homing. Both quest and goal become paradigmatic (RK).

Awake, Awakening

inhale, enact
the crappy sun

or face
finagle

far, and the body
wait

(the blackfoot had
no names for days)

the banjo, call
clairvoyant, still

gesticulate
triumphant

strum
and the morning

first, archaic
be, become

wrong or alone
we live, in delay's body

bone, altering
bone

after the word (after
which there can be no after)

cart
and the whipped horse

I lick your nipples
with my hand

5

The bindertwine of place—
The mansource of the man—
The natural odour of the stinkweed—
The ache at the root of
*   the spinal thrust—

(Despair is   not writing the poem
say what you will about despair.)

---

*Surely this is where the original version of the poem (1969) fails (Ron Smith of Oolichan Books on Vancouver Island, pointing to the reliance on dashes—the poet, come to a crucial moment in the journey, hesitating to write the longish poem the occasion dictates. The westward (and return) journey that fascinates Kroetsch is here turned entirely into implication without adequate substance (i.e., ground), into, at best, intertext . . . Only later do three couplets suggest themselves, relating the journey to the poet's equal fascination with the visit to the land of the dead (in search of?)—

(interior, the
dark shore)

the godfish
hole

the bait bait, and
the hung hook hang

—but it is too late now, too late to weld such post-surreal niceties into a voice that in the sixties insisted on a source that was at once oral and local (RK).

Weather Vane

muse
I figure

hold us, cock and after
after the hot sun

clydesdale or
and forecast if

under adam's gun
we live

or dithyramb
of sorts, allow

self, portraying
self

think you think
the globe round

the cupola
to deem or dream

trajectory
of ignorance

(the bent pine
resisting west)

wind, swing
the arrow's edge

6

What I took to be an eagle
turned out to be a gull.
We glimpsed the sea.
The road ended

←

but it did not end:
the crying gulls turned
on the moon. The moon
was in the sea.
Despair that had sought the moon's
meaning found now the moon.
(Mile Zero is everywhere.)
The roar of the sea was the sea's roar.

1969/1981
Binghamton/Winnipeg

the story of the poem
become
the poem of the story
become

Collected Poem

Every year is the same:
it's different.

visions of
exactitude

Death is a live
issue.

The world is   always
ending.

When you get to the
beginning   stop.

Green apples make you
shit like a bird, or

once in a while, just over
the next low hill

legs are longer than arms with
few exceptions

why doesn't bogus
rhyme with slump

I want to see one square
cloud.

(tempus
forgets)

The tree is there every morning.
Maybe you noticed that too.

SOUNDING THE NAME

Sonnet #1

my first (my second) garden:
the primordial: nothingness.
Out of which.
The undomesticated.

not bad. Not bad for
a start: the garden
again, here,   north,
(of) America   not

bad for a start, a snow
white page,   and this our
daily, this every: come, muse
find me my (singing): the red-winged

blackbird   by the slough
(in spring)   perched
on a dead cattail

(resist   the temptation
to give it form   resist
the temptation   )

Birthday: June 26, 1983

In the snapshot my mother is seventeen.
She is standing beside an empty chair.
Today is my birthday, I am fifty-six.
I seat myself in the empty chair

in the snapshot. My mother is standing
against the wall of a wooden house. The
wall of the house is shingled. To her
right, and behind the chair, is a window.

I am in the house, out of sight, hiding,
so that she won't remember I am not yet
born. Her waiting eyes contain my eyes.
Her mouth, almost smiling, contains mine.

The window reflects the images of the trees
that are in the yard. I am out in the yard,
playing. I am not yet her son.

In this poem I rehearse my mother.
I hold the snapshot in my hands.
I become her approaching lover.

I'm Getting Old Now

I'm getting old now, I can tell. I dream
a lot of my mother. In my dream last night
she was in the garden, over the hill,
behind our house. She was standing. I was

playing in the pea vines. We were both happy.
Neither of us would move, in the dream. Perhaps
I wasn't playing. I was kneeling to pick peas.
My mother held in her apron the peas

we had picked together. She was standing still.
I knew she was watching me. She was
watching me grow. Like a bad weed, she liked
to say. That pleased her.

I'm getting old now. I wouldn't say I'm happy.
Serene is an adequate word. Death is not quite
the enemy it was. It is a kind of watching.

Death begins to seem a friend that one has almost
forgotten, then remembers again. In my dream,
last night, I was playing in the garden.

Sounding the Name

In this poem my mother is not dead.
The phone does not ring that October
morning of my fourteenth year.
The anonymous voice on the phone

does not say, Call Arthur to the phone.
Our hired man, a neighbour's son, quiet,
unpretentious, a man from the river hills
near our farm, does not turn from the phone,

he does not say, seeming to stress the time,
Your mother died at ten o'clock. My sister and I
do not look at each other, do not smile,
assuring each other (forever) that words are
pretenders.

In this poem my mother is not dead,
she is in the kitchen, finishing the October
canning. I am helping in the kitchen.

I wash the cucumbers. My mother asks me
to go pick some dill. The ducks are migrating.
I forget to close the garden gate.

Sonnet #5

nothing

but

nothing
but
darkness
outside my
window

nothing
but

darkness

outside

my window

nothing but
darkness

the shape of
water

Sonnet for My Daughters

I think of sloughs
in early fall, the ducks
inside the darkness,
all night, talking.

In this poem my mother
stands at the window. We
listen. She names
the birds.

The birds are talking.
The phone does not ring.
There are no messages.
No one is absent.

There are mallards and
pintails, in the dark.
My mother, listening,
names their talking.

The ducks, in the sloughs,
are part of the weather.

Eli Mandel

MINOTAUR II

My father was always out in the garage
building a shining wing, a wing
that curved and flew along the edge of blue air
in that streamed and sunlit room
that smelled of oil and engines
and crankcase grease, and especially
the lemon smell of polish and cedar.
Outside there were sharp rocks, and trees,
cold air where birds fell like rocks
and screams, hawks, kites, and cranes.
The air was filled with a buzzing and flying
and the invisible hum of a bee's wings was honey
in my father's framed and engined mind.
Last Saturday we saw him at the horizon
screaming like a hawk as he fell into the sun.

NOTES FROM THE UNDERGROUND

A woman built herself a cave
    and furnished it with torn machines
    and tree-shaped trunks and dictionaries.
Out of the town where she sprang
    to her cave of rusting texts and springs
    rushed fables of indifferent rape
    and children slain indifferently
    and daily blood.

Would you believe how free I have become
    with lusting after her?
                                        That I have become
    a melodramatist, my friends ashamed?

I have seen by the light of her burning texts
    how the indifferent blood drips
    from the brass mouths of my friends,
    how at the same table I have supped
    and grown fat.

Her breasts are planets in a reedy slough.
Lie down beside that slough awhile
    and taste the bitter reeds.

Read in the water how a drowning man
    sings of a free green life.

IN THE CAVES OF MY CITY

If I said that in the caves of our city
I have seen these eyes glare, and the bent gaze
like a pin, or a sun orbiting a dark and silent moon,
and the clenched brow, a fist like Job's or Blake's
to hammer iron language into shape
                                                or that the mouth
roared like the rustle of paper, or the sigh of elms
sick with the dutch disease, or the sound made by dikes
at the thought of the sea piling its green lava
onto the hissing towns,
                                    would you then shrug
and say: animals have visions, the beast
is not at ease until he's clean.
                                            Dirt?
You look at your nails: the horns of Jericho,
Joshua once clawed down walls, Isaiah shrieked

a mouthful of dikes at Leviathan (hooked him
on a simile shaped like a beak, hung him
on its barb).
                    The word. I see her summer dress
lift, in the white of her skin, a leprous snow,
the red slash of the sun smiles below
her bruised blue brow.
                                        Must I become Chaplin
to praise and save her? My tongue flickers
like a newsreel, and with epileptic grace
I lurch through the twenties of my mind,
a celluloid hero, fabulous as a Basilisk
who pins me in the caves of my city.

THE GOLD BUG

a poisonous bee burst his pod
in the palm of my hand
                                        his venom

flowed over my hand like honey

now honoured among men
I gesture with my golden hand
and speak with the language of money

HALLOWE'EN BY ST. MARY'S CONVENT

A whitewashed wall.
Two shadows of a single nun
pass and repass vine, wall, vine again.
Time gathers the plucked fruit
in a heaped sunlight of gourds.

Gourds
　　　multiple as the sun
　　　eclipsed on coloured film
　　　climb the white and darkening
　　　shadow of the wall.

Streetlights blossom on their stems.
Like honeybees in lust of bloom
small Spirits hum through meadows of the dark
toward the petalled homes, the flowered rooms.
And out of Revelation, Angels swarm
to feed on spiritual sweet food,
globed fruit, round nut, and jelly bean.

Such occult cheerfulness the swarm
exudes from sticky maiche of skull
and sheeted ghost, gusty with laugh,
as makes them guest, forgives the child
his candle in the skull, forgives
his blinded eye, his idiotic grin,
all ills of flesh unmasked by mask on flesh.

CITY PARK MERRY-GO-ROUND

Freedom is seldom what you now believe.
Mostly you circle round and round the park:
Night follows day, these horses never leave.

Like children, love whatever you conceive,
See then your world as lights whirled in the dark.
Freedom is seldom what you now believe.

Your world moves up and down or seems to weave
And still you pass you pass the same ringed mark.
Night follows day, these horses never leave.

You thought your past was here, you might retrieve
That wild illusion whirling in the dark.
Freedom is seldom what you now believe.

Sick on that circle you begin to grieve.
You wish the ride would end you could escape the park.
Night follows day, these horses never leave.

Mostly you circle round and round the park.
You'd give your life now to be free to leave.
Freedom is seldom what you now believe.
Night follows day, these horses never leave.

CARLETON UNIVERSITY: JANUARY 1961

To George Johnston

Imagine a speaking rock: stone-dumb
mountains lean over Ottawa
but even the dumb stone spires
of Parliament Hill aspire to speech.

There is something raucous in Ottawa:
coarse is the P.M.'s speech,
brash the Privy Council's course
between Hull and the unspeakable Laurentians.

I think of a child's yell of pain
when he is speared by malicious tables,
explanation animate, mythical, fabulous,
and then of you, articulate climber,
bruised by stony syntax
on the mountains of Gawain's English.

How many beastly tables have you slain
where Carleton and its new cement
utter a few blue nouns and glassy verbs
between the howling trains and muzzled snow?

DAY OF ATONEMENT: STANDING

My Lord, how stands it with me now
who, standing here before you
(who, fierce as you are, are also just),
cannot bow down. You order this.
Why, therefore, I must break
if bend I will not, yet bend I must.

But I address myself to you thus,
covered and alert, and will not bare
my self. Then I must bear you,
heavy as you are.
                                        This is the time
the bare tree bends in the fierce wind
and stripped, my God, springs to the sky.

DAVID

all day the gopher-killing boys
        their sling-shot arms
                their gopher-cries

the king insisting
        my poetry must stop

I have written nothing since May

instead
                walk among the boys
gopher-blood on their stretched
hands
                murder will end murder
the saying goes, someone must
do something about the rodents
and poems do not:
                                        even the doctors

admit that it's plague
ask me about my arms
                    look
at my shadow hanging
   like a slingshot

the world turns like a murderous stone
     my forehead aching with stars

THE COMEDIANS

You might have expected music
But they move so slowly they make no sound.
Like swimmers they put their large hands
Up before their huge red mouths
As if to shove mountains of water
Inches over so they can breathe.

And yet you think you hear gasps,
Snuffling, muffled yelps, occasional
Screams when one wallops the other
Or with a paddle shuffles on his enormous feet
Toward his kneeling unsuspecting friend.

Sometimes in their drowning motions
They remove their arms and heads
And walk in their bodies like barrels.

No longer do I care for those critics
Who plead with me that Whitman is God.
As for that other poet, he too was lying.
Warmed by outlandish currents
I have begun to build an aquarium
Tolerant only for tropical fish
Who move like swimmers without sound
And nuzzle one another with their golden mouths.

RAPUNZEL
Girl in a Tower

Another one of those puzzles
there's not a farmer
skinny as a gold seed
tough as a nutcracker
can plough or crack.

How do towers grow like that?
Overnight: the garden
a green sky, its moon
like beet, its sun
a turnip underground?

Many girls lock themselves up,
become pantries, closets.
Some, like trees, grow bark,
and others, like rivers,
burble into dimpled pools.

But they are not these crooked
wicked towers, not rooms
inside of rooms, not brooms
to thrash out of a seedy man
his golden crop and garden.

I lean on a ladder of hair,
remember the right rhymes,
look up at the green head,
climb toward the turnip-colour sun.

PSALM 24

I no longer want to see
those terrible corrections
underlined with the red-ink
of crab-apples bleeding on the lawn.

Take away your Talmudic trees
commenting on the stone Torah of our streets.

Isn't it enough that I've failed?
Do you have to indulge in this melodrama
of snowstorms and black poppies?

What did you expect?
You, who drove me to mad alphabets
and taught me all the wrong words.

It's your scripture. You read it.

HOUDINI

I suspect he knew that trunks are metaphors,
could distinguish between the finest rhythms
unrolled on rope or singing in a chain
and knew the metrics of the deepest pools

I think of him listening to the words
spoken by manacles, cells, handcuffs,
chests, hampers, roll-top desks, vaults,
especially the deep words spoken by coffins

escape, escape: quaint Harry in his suit
his chains, his desk, attached to all attachments
how he'd sweat in that precise struggle
with those binding words, wrapped around him
like that mannered style, his formal suit

and spoken when? by whom? What thing first said
"there's no way out"?; so that he'd free himself,
leap, squirm, no matter how, to chain himself again,
once more jump out of the deep alive
with all his chains singing around his feet
like the bound crowds who sigh, who sigh.

WABAMUN

1

lake
        holds
                sun moon stars

                trees
                    hold

stars moon sun

2

thunder
          and sky
towel
          wet sand
in yellow light

          yesterday

3

on water
many suns
            here there
fires then

silent comedians
gulls
perch jumping

4

only
      waves   motion
      sun   dancing

no   sun

only
      light
hurting
in its
      endless
dance

5

each day I
step
      farther
into dark water

once I will
know
        no longer

whether
            that one
floating
            is myself
or the light
                 one
standing
             on the red
pier

6

moon train on causeway

coal cars

a white moon

7

to have come to this
simplicity
to know
only
the absolute
calm
lake

before

night

8

clover   smell
sweet stars in a green sky

white sweet stars
blossom in a green sky

clover   stars
in a white sky

white
stars

LISTEN, THE SEA

yes what is
I'm learning

by your leave
leaving
            rising
to leave
            return
and turn
            we
deliberate
by the waves
rhythm casual
move
           tidal
as
       traffic
as
   the sea-women

neither are they
certain uncertain
but with us
                withal
within
           their song
here
       oh hear
it is

READING ROOM: PERIODICALS
(also in the annotations of Borges)

seeing he was blind, said: please
clarify systems involved in voice over
and the animation of Walter Cronkite
said in voice over this event is random
do not accept   do not accept
if the seal is broken the unidentified
black object or the unidentified green

and after this looked: a door opened
and a voice said—it was a voice
like Dustin Hoffman's playing Jack
Crabb the oldest man in the world who
really killed Custer said I will give
you a book and in voice over said
do not accept if the seal is broken

and a voice said
                    this is an
autoclock transcript abridged version
this is
      a random event stop clock stop
clock   there has been a real
time loss subject has given uncodeable
response
           end
print
        end print
        no change
        programme

                        ends

FIRST POLITICAL SPEECH

first, in the first place, to begin with, secondly,
in the second place, lastly

again, also, in the next place, once more, moreover,
furthermore, likewise, besides, similarly, for example,
for instance, another

then, nevertheless, still, however, at the same time,
yet, in spite of that, on the other hand, on the contrary

certainly, surely, doubtless, indeed, perhaps, possibly,
probably, anyway, in all probability, in all likelihood,
at all events, in any case

therefore, consequently, accordingly, thus, as a result,
in consequence of this, as might be expected

the foregoing, the preceding, as previously mentioned

as already stated

Transition Table
from **Learning to Write** *by Ernest H. Winter*
(Second Revised Edition) Macmillan
(Toronto, 1961), p. 156

ON THE 25TH ANNIVERSARY OF THE LIBERATION OF AUSCHWITZ:

Memorial Services, Toronto, January 25, 1970
YMHA Bloor & Spadina

the name is hard
a German sound made out of
the gut gutteral throat
y scream yell ing open
voice mouth growl
                                        and sweat
"the only way out of Auschwitz
is through the chimneys"
                                                  of course
that's second hand   that's told
again   Sigmund Sherwood (Sobolewski)
twisting himself into that sentence
before us on the platform
                                                       the poem
shaping itself late in the after
noon later than it would be:

Pendericki's "Wrath of God"
moaning electronic Polish theatric
the screen silent
                              framed by the name
looking away from/pretending not there
no name no not name no

               Auschwitz
          in GOTHIC lettering
                                                       the hall
a parody a reminiscence a nasty memory
the Orpheum in Estevan before Buck Jones
the Capitol in Regina before Tom Mix
waiting for the guns

waiting for the cowboy killers
one two three
                    Legionnaires
Polish ex-prisoners Association
Legions
            their medals their flags

so the procession, the poem gradual
ly insistent beginning to shape itself
with the others
                    walked with them
into the YMHA Bloor & Spadina
thinking apocalypse shame degradation
thinking bones and bodies melting
thickening thinning melting bones and bodies
thinking not mine / must speak clearly
the poet's words / Yevtyshenko at Baba-Yar

there this January snow
heavy wet the wind heavy wet
the street grey white slush melted concrete
bones and bodies melting slush
                                                saw
with the others
                    the prisoner
in the YMHA hall Bloor & Spadina
arms wax stiff body stiff unnatural
coloured face blank eyes
                                        walked
with the others toward the screen
toward the picture
                                    SLIDES
                    this is mother
                    this is father
                    this is
                            the one who is
waving her arms like that

is the one who
                        like
I mean running with her breasts bound
ing
      running
                     with her hands here and there
with her here and
                            there
hands
        that   that is
the poem becoming the body
becoming the faint hunger
ing body
               prowling
                              through
words the words words the words
opening   mouths ovens
the generals smiling saluting
in their mythic uniforms god-like
generals uniforms with the black leather
with the straps and the intricate leather
the phylacteries and the prayer shawl
corsets and the boots and the leather straps

and the shining faces of the generals in their boots
and their stiff wax bodies their unnatural faces
and their blank eyes and their hands their stiff hands
and the generals in their straps and wax and stiff
staying standing
                            melting bodies and thickening
                            quick flesh on flesh handling
                            hands
        the poem flickers, fades
the four Yarzeit candles guttering   one
        each four million lights dim
my words drift
                smoke from chimneys and ovens

a bad picture, the power failing
pianist clattering on and over and through
the long Saturday afternoon in the Orpheum
while the whitehatted star spangled cowboys
shot the dark men and shot the dark men
and we threw popcorn balls and grabbed
each other and cheered:
me jewboy yelling
for the shot town and the falling men
and the lights come on
and
with the others
standing in silence

the gothic word hangs
over us on a shroud-white screen

and we drift away
to ourselves
to the late Sunday Times
the wet snow
the city

a body melting

FROM "THE PENTAGON PAPERS"

Glossary:

AA	CAT	DIA	EPTEL (Deptel/Septel?)	
AAA	CHICOM	DOD		
AID	CHINAT			FAL
ASA	CHMAAG			FAR
ABM	CIAP			FEC
AMB	CINCPAC			FMWA
ASAP	COMUSMACV			FY
				FYI
		LOC	MAAG	PACON

ICA MAC POLAD
ICC KIA MAP
I MDAP QTE
IDA
ISA

ROK RSM RSSZ RTA RVNAFRVNA SAC SAM SAR
SMMSNIESTCSVNTAORTERMTETTFTO&ETRIMUNO
USAFUSGUSIAUSIBUSISUSOMUWVCVMVNVNAFVOA
WTYT

UNQTE

ROLLING THUNDER

BARREL ROLL

BLUE SPRINGS FARMGATE FLAMING DART LEAPING LENA

The Trilemma:

a. Will-breaking strikes on the North (para 7) are balked by (1) flash-point limits, (2) by doubts that DRV will cave and (3) by doubts that VC will obey caving DRV

b. Large U.S. troop deployments. (para 9) are blocked by "French-defeat" and "Korea" syndromes, and Quat is queasy. (Troops could be net negatives, and be beseiged).

c. Exit by negotiations (para 9) is tainted by the humiliation likely to follow.

insurrection defection dissension impotence defeat-
ism concession accommodation

deployment of Frogs and Sams in North Vietnam
hot pursuit flak suppression strike strikes strikes
risks:
losses panic revulsion sympathetic fires over
Berlin, Cyprus, Kashmir, Jordan waters

stretch-out retard the program
circuit breaker
                    shunt

BIRTHMARK:

seeing a mouse
my mother struck her temple

he'll be marked at birth
she said
          the women cried

I carry the souris
on my brow
               the river
in my head
               the valley
of my dreams
still echoes
with her cry

ESTEVAN, 1934:

remembering the family we
called breeds   the Roques
their house smelling of urine
my mother's prayers before
the dried fish she cursed
them for their dirtiness their
women I remember too
                              how
seldom they spoke and
they touched one another

even when the sun killed
cattle and rabbis
even
in poisoned slow air
like hunters
like lizards
they touched stone
they touched
earth

RETURNING FROM WAR:

for jbm 1918-1944

floors gleaming in the white frame house
yellow as wax the night before he died
she said her eyes yellow as a hawk's
she saw him dressed in white clean
she said this in the room the blinds
drawn heat leaning on the house
over the room's dusk the floor's gleam
white he was so clean

in the estevan summer
hazardous as desert hear
gopher squeaks momentary hawks
lean in the pushing and shoving
wind the sun breathing
heat
and the impossibility of death

THE CROOKED GODS:

the crooked gods:

do they mean anything?
I ask Ann
          parkland
rolling below sandstone

silent
        she turns
the camera
            here
there
        I kneel
before the crooked gods

last night wheeling
over the land
their handprints
their great feet
their stone faces
move
        turning
we leave
take with us
photographs
silent
        as
their open mouths

GOING TO PIECES

First I begin to notice my sweater has unravelled.
Then it becomes obvious my trousers no longer fit as they used to.
Heels on new shoes have worn down.
No one tells me about my hair's length,
the rash on my unshaven face, my bleared eyes,
glasses through which I can barely see
smeared as they are with marmalade, toast crumbs, and blood,
the egg stains on my moustache, my wife saying she'll leave me
for a younger man or at least a better poet, my children away
in anger or despair. Lately, I've taken to plans to
swim, a Cheever hero, from pool to pool,
one county to the next, in the darkening afternoon,
toward my house now turned gothic stable with pigs and bears.

Oh the changes that happen. My body: parts of it
outside of me now like an old shoe
attached to my left hand, leathery and unwelcome, my visible liver,
white mould I thought attractive greying hair in fact brain cells.
I'm turning inside out, all the secrets spilled in the open
as if the poems I couldn't write took shape anyhow: pieces of imagery
stuck to my skin and hair, unused lines trickling from the corners of
my eyes and mouth, wrinkles of sonnets
mapping a face of wrecked words, the unintelligible damage of poetry
I couldn't use for vitamins, scurvy of lost language.

John Newlove

FUNERAL

So she said to me, my
mother that is, or
whoever you like, riding
out to the cemetery in the

slow rain, the comfortable car,
she said, Don't
cry, don't show anything, don't,
don't let them see it,

and the priest stood there, who
later died of cancer, and
was so mild, coughing
prayers in his black cassock,

(and what my uncle said is
a different matter), she
said, Don't expose yourself,
don't let them laugh.

IN THE FOREST

In the forest
down the cut roads
the sides of them
gravel rolls
thundering down,
each small stone
a rock waterfall
that frightens me
sitting in my ditch.

I smoke my last
cigarette rolled
with bible paper,
listen to the stone
cascading down,
some of it bouncing
off my hunched shoulders.
Above me the dark grass
hangs over the edge
like a badly-fitted wig—
10 feet above me.

I dream of the animals
that may sulk there,
deer snake and bear
dangerous and inviolable
as I am not inviolable.
Even the gentle deer
scare me at midnight,
no one else for 100 miles,
even the sucking snakes
small and lithe as syrup.
The forest is not silent,
water smashes its way,
rocks bounce, wind magnifies

its usual noise
and my shivering fear
makes something alive
move in the trees,
shift in the grass
10 feet above me.

I am too frightened
to move or to stay,
sweating in the wind.
An hour later
I convulse unthinking,
and run, run, run down the cold road.

SUSAN 4

In winter at least
the woman's arms went
round me from the back
as she kissed, making me
feel better so that I

immediately danced (and
I am very awkward) down
the basement stairs in
sandals and

threw three shovelfuls of soft
expensive coal onto the rickety
pernickety old iron furnace
to celebrate this
wifely favour.

VERIGIN III

The pure white bodies of my friends,
d'un blanc pur, like—
like a cigarette paper! shivering

in cold spring before a cold
shallow waterhole. Thin naked
bodies, ribs, knees, buttocks, hearts,

young bilingual doukhobors,
where are you now? I cut my foot
on a piece of rusty tin and walked
home alone, shoe full of blood.

NO PLEASURE

There is no pleasure anywhere.
The zinc air stinks
with a persistent pain. Cheap drugs
rain into the stomach,
becoming mud. The tug
of gravity produces cramps;
I lug myself along like a garden slug
in this damp bed. Nothing I'd read
prepared me for a body this unfair.

As I lift up a coffeecup
I hear the shoulder's intimation
with common fear: I will rip you,
my muscles are on you. And the back too
slips in: Do not bend or I will fit
into your sleep tonight and wake you up
with frightened cramps; there are ramps
into a sea down which we can drive you,
with no one there to shrive you.

Forming letters with a pen
when this treachery
reaches me is my only male answer:
trying not to be
immediate, but in some way elegant
by hand—something my corpse
can't do. But even here
the styleless jerk intrudes,
and I am left alone with it again.

LAST SUMMER A NUMBER OF OUR PEOPLE DIED JUST FOR A WANT OF SOMETHING TO LIVE ON

We have got in a country where we do not find all
as stated to us when we was asked
to swap lands with you
and we do not get as much as promised us
at the treaty of St Marys neither. . . .

Father—We did not think that big man
would tell us things that was not true. We have found
a poor hilly stony country and the worst of all
no game to be found on it to live on.

Last summer our corn looked very well
until a heavy rain come on for 3 or 4 days
and raised the waters
so high that we could just see
the tops of our corn in some of the fields and it
destroyed the greatest part of our corn, punkins and beans
and a great many more of my people coming on
and we had to divide our little stock with them.

Last summer there was a few deere here and we had a few hogs
but we was obliged to kill all of them
and some that was not our own
but this summer there are no game nor no hogs
and my old people and children must suffer.

Father—You know its hard to be hungry,
if you do not know it we poor Indians know it.
Father—If we go a great ways off we may find some deere
but if we do that
we cannot make any corn
and we still must suffer.
Father—We are obliged to call on you
onst more for assistance in the name of God. . . .

Father—We expect a great many more of our people
here this spring to make corn . . . we wish to gether
all of my people onst more to Gether
cass I know I cant live always; Father—

> Found in Grant Foreman's *Indians and Pioneers*, University of Oklahoma Press, 1936, pp. 197-8, quoting from the U.S. Office of Indian Affairs Retired Classified Files "1824, *Delaware on White River.*" The letter was written by the Delaware to General Clark, February, 1824.

MY DADDY DROWNED

My daddy drowned still blind kittens
in the rainbarrel corner of our white house
& I make poems babies & love-affairs
out of women I've only seen once

or maybe never at all. Daddy
had to push those kittens under in a sack
to keep them from squealing & I don't know
whether he hated or enjoyed it; no expression

was permitted to cross his legal face. I'm
the same way, Freud says so, I let
no expression on my lips when I read,

pushing those women underneath
to drown in poems. It's one way
to get them down. But I wonder about daddy,
if he's the same as me,
                                        because sometimes
I let those women slip to the surface
& squeak a little bit before I kill them.

NOT MOVING

Waterfalls
in the dark
& the noise

very much

      the animals
      undoubtedly
      moving there
      & waiting

rocks
rolling down
the gravel
cuts
of the road

      there
      bears be
      pack rats (curious
      to see (snakes
      lizards

deer moving
among
the trees
quietly

also
on the side
of the road
me

smoking
nervously
at midnight
100 miles
to go

& cold
& afraid
on the side of the road

the only animal

not moving
at all.

THE SINGING HEAD

The singing head that
does not falter when
it falls

but sings for seven
short years more, or nine,

or for as long
as it may be lucky
to shout out the words
in measured time

or to the ear's delight
to hear

the auditory
nerves carry on
the sound,

the self-made sound
the mouth manufactured

of the air,
of the endless
chant of praised delight

that could
not feel the sword or
cry to feel its hot
blood gush

where the neck had led
to the carolling lungs
and balanced body tilting

in the wind, the head
in grass or just

tossed under any bush
or muddled in a ditch . . .

it carries on
to raise its breathless voice,
to praise

the life that while it lived
was good, to praise
the grass
or bush or muddy ditch,

that where it stays
is good.

VERIGIN, MOVING IN ALONE

fatherless, 250 people
counting dogs and gophers
we would say, Jmaeff's grocerystore,
me in grade 4, mother
principal of the 2-building
3-room 12-grade school,

a boy sitting on the grass
of a small hill, the hot fall,
speaking no russian, an airgun
my sister gave me making me envied.

I tried all fall, all spring
the next ominous year, to kill
a crow with it, secretly glad
I could not, the men
in winter shooting the town's
wild dogs, casually tossing
the quick-frozen, barely-bleeding
head-shot corpses onto
the street-side snowbanks,

the highway crews cutting their way
through to open the road with what
I was sure was simply
some alternate of a golden summer's
wheat-threshing machine, children
running through the hard-tossed spray,
pretending war from the monster's snout,

leaping into snowbanks
from Peter The Lordly Verigin's
palace on the edge of town
in a wild 3-dimensional
cubistic game of cops and robbers,

cold spring swimming
in Dead Horse Creek and farmers' dugouts
and doomed fishing
in beastless ponds, strapped
in school for watching a fight,

coldly holding back tears
and digging for drunken father's
rum-bottle, he had finally
arrived, how I loved him,
loved him, love him, dead, still.

My mad brother chased me
alone in the house with him
around and around
the small living room, airgun,
rifle in hand, silently
our breaths coming together—

RIDE OFF ANY HORIZON

Ride off any horizon
and let the measure fall
where it may—

on the hot wheat,
on the dark yellow fields
of wild mustard, the fields

of bad farmers, on the river,
on the dirty river full
of boys and on the throbbing

powerhouse and the low dam
of cheap cement and rocks
boiling with white water,

and on the cows and their powerful
bulls, the heavy tracks
filling with liquid at the edge

of the narrow prairie
river running steadily away.

✧

Ride off any horizon
and let the measure fall
where it may—

among the piles of bones
that dot the prairie

in vision and history
(the buffalo and deer,

dead indians, dead settlers,
the frames of lost houses

left behind in the dust
of the depression,

dry and profound, that
will come again in the land

and in the spirit, the land
shifting and the minds

blown dry and empty—
I have not seen it! except

in pictures and talk—
but there is the fence

covered with dust, laden,
the wrecked house stupidly empty)—

here is a picture for your wallet,
of the beaten farmer and his wife
leaning toward each other—

sadly smiling, and emptied of desire.

Ride off any horizon
and let the measure fall
where it may—

off the edge
of the black prairie

as you thought you could fall,
a boy at sunset

not watching the sun
set but watching the black earth,

never-ending they said in school,
round: but you saw it ending,

finished, definite, precise—
visible only miles away.

Ride off any horizon
and let the measure fall
where it may—

on a hot night the town
is in the streets—

the boys and girls
are practising against

each other, the men
talk and eye the girls,

the women talk and
eye each other, the indians
play pool: eye on the ball.

✧

Ride off any horizon
and let the measure fall
where it may—

and damn the troops, the horsemen
are wheeling in the sunshine,
the cree, practising

for their deaths: mr poundmaker,
gentle sweet mr big bear,
it is not unfortunately

quite enough to be innocent,
it is not enough merely
not to offend—

at times to be born
is enough, to be
in the way is too much—

some colonel otter, some
major-general middleton will
get you, you—

indian. It is no good to say,
I would rather die
at once than be in that place—

though you love that land more,
you will go where they take you.

✧

Ride off any horizon
and let the measure fall—

where it may;
it doesn't have to be

the prairie. It could be
the cold soul of the cities
blown empty by commerce

and desiring commerce
to fill up the emptiness.

The streets are full of people.

It is night, the lights
are on; the wind

blows as far as it may. The streets
are dark and full of people.

Their eyes are fixed as far as
they can see beyond each other—

to the concrete horizon, definite,
tall against the mountains,
stopping vision visibly.

INDIAN WOMEN

Saturday night
kamsack is
something
to lie about,

the streets full
of indians and
doukhobors,
raw men and

fat women (watch
out for
the women people
said, all the men

do is drink
beer and play
pool but watch
out for those

indian women),
cars
driving up
and down the

main street
from the new
high school

building to
the cn
station and
back

again, paved
road where
the rest were
only oiled

gravel in
the good
old summer

time, in the good
old summertime,
son, when
everybody who

was nobody was
out on the street
with a belly

full talking
to beat
hell and
the heat.

PUBLIC LIBRARY

So I sat day after day in the smoking room of the library
some book or paper or magazine on my knee
smoking   half reading
half in a dreamed trance   half listening
to the sounds around me   half looking
at the people around me

the sounds   shuffling of canvas covered feet
rubber soled feet   moccasined feet
newspapers being borrowed   being shaken
rustling like a sea or wind
sea of other peoples' lives
wind a movement of other peoples' air and breathing
books crackling as their backs were broken
the flick/flick of fingertips
and fingernails on the corners of pages
snap of shutting decisively

or accidentally   plump lackadaisically
muted thump of being tossed on low tables
abandoned as too boring
having small type and big ideas or big type and small ideas
magazines slapping against other magazines
heavy glossy pages scraping and sliding against each other
pieces of paper being torn   irritating noise
magnification of a snail's death scream
being stepped on   and the sounds of the people

snores grunts slobbers   sighs
aimless and tuneless humming
toneless and breathless whispering of unknown tunes
noise of the man who sat all day
from nine-thirty in the morning until nine at night
going   aaah aaah   every four seconds
the man who blew his nose noisily between his fingertips
ten times an hour
and snapped the slime off his hand   slap
the asthmatic breathing of another
the man who talked to himself
in a strange sounding language
something slavic or made up
giggling and twittering between the phrases
his laughter rising as the day went on
to a higher and higher more hysterical pitch
until when it seemed he would finally have to collapse
from giggling he suddenly flushed
as if insulted by himself
and screamed in english   the anguish language
Son of a bitch   son of a bitch you
put on his hat and left to go home and make supper
for himself in some grey room

old men snorting in bewildered hurt derision at the newspapers
and trying to suck up the mucus in their noses
without having to show a dirty handkerchief

so strong their pride
feeling passed by   abandoned
left alone by all the other billions
matches being drawn along plaster walls
scraping like magazine pages
small explosions of wooden matches
cigarettes lustily sucked on
cigarettes thrown on the floor
cigarettes ground out with hate on the floor
revenge against old men's diseases
cancer possibilities   against the all night
long coughing and spitting themselves
and the neighbours' coughing and spitting also

people   in canvas shoes   rubber soles
loggers' boots   years-old oxfords with great cavities
moccasins   thick grey woollen socks knee high
old army issue from two wars at least
baggy cuffless pants   cotton workshirts
flannel plaids sweated in for twenty summers and winters
brassbound army and police suspenders
mismatched doublebreasted fantastically wide lapelled
old pointed blue pinstripe suitcoats
relics of other generations   the wearers outside
all generations   other excitements   dancing
polkas in the northland or on the prairies
to screechy violins and accordions
heavy brown horsey overcoats pulling down their thin shoulders
white beard stubble with tobacco stains
grey beard stubble   white hair
grey hair   trembly hands   rheumy eyes
pale watery eyes   shallow ponds
huge bulging veins popping out from necks and foreheads
glasses with cracked lenses

only here and there the younger ones within twenty years of me
a little neater   the hair still coloured
dull the veins
and breathing and spit a little less obvious
a hint of combs and razor blades
and rarely the well-dressed
tightly-girdle-assed pointy-wire-breasted and well-stroked
young woman would come in and look about
as if she had blundered into the wrong toilet
afraid to walk out again immediately
lest we be too obviously insulted

choosing a chair   trying to look unconcerned
lighting a cigarette   sitting in her stiff brassière
with all the men who could see far enough staring furtively
at her fat knees   shifting around in their chairs
to ease the strain on the crotches of their greasy pants
as forgotten juices stirred

—when her cigarette was half smoked the woman
girl that is   would butt it in the ashtray   fold
her book   carefully preserving the place
and leave for a safer floor on the building
one where she would not feel those shifty eyes
on her breasts   eyes on her legs
evil male eyes endeavouring to see up her
tight skirts   to see her sweating thighs
to see

and sometimes heavy businessmen
come in and blunder out again
like cardiac bears
but of them
I will not speak for I do not know.

THE PRAIRIE

One compiles, piles, plies
these masses of words, verbs,
massifs, mastiffs barking meaning,
dried chips
of buffalo dung, excreta from beasts

the prairie fed, foddered,
food for generations: men roaming
as beasts seen through dips
in history, fostered by legend,
invented remembrance. Scenes shake,

the words do not suffice. One bred
on the same earth wishes himself
something different, the other's
twin, impossible thing, twining
both memories, a double meaning,

but cannot be—never
to be at ease, but always migrating
from city to city
seeking some almost seen
god or food or earth or word.

THE CAVE

The stars are your deathbed.
You rest from the cave
to Pluto or whatever dark planets
lie beyond. No ideas trap you.

In the unobstructed sunlight miles high
the Earth is beautiful as a postcard.
Sinai looks as the map says it should,
and people are too small to be observed.

In Africa there are no trees to see.
It is a map world.
The sunlight is brilliant
as a two-carat diamond on a girl's hand.

The girl is young, visible to your mind,
growing older. Beyond Pluto
and the darkest planets, children surround her.

The diamond glows on her finger
like a worm. The stars, the stars
shine like one-carat diamonds. Beyond
Pluto and the darkest planets the stars shine.

The diamonds shine in wormy rings
on fingers, in coffins of unobstructed space.
The flesh circles the bone in strips
in the coffin as the ring circled flesh.

The two-carat sun hangs loosely,
just restraining the Earth. Beyond the planets,
beyond the dark coffin, beyond the ring of stars,
your bed is in the shining, tree-lit cave.

WHAT TO DREAM ABOUT

How long does it take you to decide
what to dream about? Do you think
carefully beforehand of women
you never enjoyed and who
would never agree to enjoy you?

Do you desire to dream of the deaths
of those you love so your sorrow
will be splendid among your friends?

Do you carefully build in your mind
your own car crash the police will announce
in tones that know your loss so well?

Do you rehearse your best tragedies,
distilling them into your dreams
night after night before your sleep,
your hair growing grey in your bed,
your pleasant tears huge on your head?

Or do you dream of a real loss,
the bent caverns of the dark sea,
the glass trees rough, shining at night,
no other animal in sight?

Glen Sorestad

(AT BATOCHE, JUNE 1975)

during those sky-filled days in may
ninety years ago on this same height of land
perhaps middleton stood at this very spot
viewed the twisting river under this same sky
and issued the orders to dig the rifle pits
which my boys now regard with faint curiosity
and just maybe the afternoon was as quiet
as it is now, still as gunner phillip's grave
just down the slope toward the muddy water
"where are all the other soldiers' graves?"
my youngest son asks and i tell him
that this war did not claim thousands
but i don't think it makes much sense to him
because it's not like that on television
        and when he asks what they were fighting about
        it's hard to explain to him how a metis nation
        was stillborn ninety years ago on this river
        and i have this feeling that he thinks it's all
        some sort of hoax because he knows that no toys
        are sold at christmas, replicas of middleton
        or dumont, no plastic metis, cree or grenadiers
        so how could a battle have occurred here
        and not be refought in comics, on television
        or perpetuated in games by parker or ideal?
        even the bullet holes of the gatling gun
        that pock the church rectory at batoche
        must seem suspiciously to a small boy
        like the work of woodpeckers

in the cemetery at batoche lie metis
and descendants of the originals
who trekked across the prairie grasses
following the dwindling buffalo
until the last shot was fired
and the dusty herds were no more
at batoche along the south saskatchewan
they turned to grub-hoe and axe
their names still prominent along the roads
mailboxes of metis history—
oulette, desjarlais, pilon, fiddler—
chiseled in gravestone
near the church of st. antoine de padoue
overlooking the river
five small headstones stand together
near the fence's edge
and my boys read the tragedy of the date
five children at once
"was it during the war, daddy?"
the youngest asks
and i have to tell him no
it wasn't war at all
probably a fire at night
that claimed them
(though it was every bit as final
as a gatling gun)
and maybe i should have said yes . . .
what does it matter?
wars and battles and death
to sun-alive children
are all just as remote and abstract
under a blazing june sky
the air singing and smelling of life

HOMESTEAD

for Ellend Dalshaug

1903. Ride the CPR to Yorkton, end of the line.
The Doukhobors are already ahead. Four years.
Walk north by west. Buy wagons, horses, grandfather.
(If you can. They're going fast, the price is climbing.)
Move to the land, north-west to Buchanan—
unknown name in an unknown land
past Good Spirit Lake, twelve miles of water
that teems with ever-hungry pike.
Camp on the sand dunes and rest a while.

Claim the land, build the log shack, chinked with mud.
Hew the poplar stands, the willow thickets
the hazel nut, saskatoons, chokecherry bushes.
Hone the axe's edge, grandfather
for the land must be cleared for wheat and oats.
Grub out the poplar roots, the willows.
Trim the straightest trees for the buildings
for many are needed—the house
a barn, sheds to come. And firewood, grandfather
for you have heard the stories about the winters.
Stack the deadfall in piles for sawing later.
Sharpen the axe again. Keep chopping.
Summer is fast fading, grandfather—
this morning the water pail was filmed with ice
and the axe rang like a yodel down a fiord.
Keep chopping, grandfather. Winter is coming
and the prairie wind breathes frost.

SHITEPOKE

for Bob Kroetsch

shikepoke / sloughpump
shike/poke   slough/pump
shitepoke   shitpoke
what does it matter now?

> shikepoke or sloughpump
> the memory fades   fades
> we name and then unname
> but it was our word   good enough
> for anyone but ornithologists
> who latinize the bird world

the plains Cree named it
moo-ku-hoo-sew
naming the evening sound
when an Indian says the name
you can smell summer slough

and the first French trader
named it *butor*   then plunged
his paddle deep to pass by

> does it really matter
> that this bird
> is really the *yellow bittern*
> (though no one I know
> ever heard or used this name)?

we didn't know that shitepoke
was some English settler's way
of naming the bird
that shits when it leaps
to flight from the slough

I can still hear
the pump-handle sound cut the evening
still mould in my throat
the shitepoke sound

shikepoke / sloughpump
you are my language   my image
shike/poke   slough/pump

BEGINNINGS

i

in the beginning there was
always the wind

tearing the ears

ii

wind and sun
hammer verbs
into the brain

later you learn
the language
of frost   blackening
leaves of summer

the sounds
of spring's entrance
dropping slowly
from the eaves

in the night
the call of the geese
flowing overhead
against silent stars

iii

around the quarter-section
barbed wire loops and sags
from rotting willow posts
mauled into the stubborn earth
by sledge and sweat

now   long after
the cattle have been sold
white-tailed deer
pause
gather limbs to leap
over this rusting confine

iv

the poem is not so much
the rusted knots of wire
that bound the prairie mind

it is the impaled wing
the sole reminder
of a sharp-tailed grouse
that flaps now on the wire
like some unremembered
signal

v

in the dark coulee buckbrush
thorns are words
to slash the tongue
rip away the softness
of autumn sunlight

ALEXANDRA

Twenty years forgetting can
never wipe our memories clean.

Newspapers forget. Telecasts can
not outlive each day's new killings.

The beauty contest you won is forgotten.
The patients you nursed are well, or dead.

The river grasses no longer hear
the screaming in your blood.

The police have found new mysteries,
new bloodlettings, new victims.

But somewhere a tormented man
sits in darkness of his own,

and no river can wash from his mind
the slow flow of your dying.

He can not twist his hands enough
to wipe the feel of your flesh away.

Each day your face will grow
younger in his album of dark recall

until the day he will believe
it love and must tell all.

BACKYARD MOMENT

for Ray Souster

The robin has just settled
into the birdbath and now
cocks its head at me
expectantly.
                Out of habit,
family man that I am,
I turn my eyes away
discreetly.

SHELLING PEAS

In the desert heat of Saskatchewan August
like exhausted dancers peas wilt by mid-day;
you must rise in the early morning to pick
the plump pods at their peak of freshness.

In the shade you sit with three containers:
the basket of peas, waiting to be depearled,
the smaller bucket for the rattle of peas,
the waste container for the emptied pods.
You take care in the placement of the three—
eliminate wasted movement, position each
to suit your handedness, minimize the time
between the plucking of the fresh pod
and expelling of the spent shell.

Your thumbnail becomes an oyster knife
to pry the shell, the thumb slides inside
the violated lips and thrums the gems
into the bucket in a green dance of hail;
the other hand flips the husks away.
In seconds it is a familiar act,
new as spring, ageless as love:

slit of thumbnail, crack of entry,
chorus of peas, snap of discards.
You slip easily into this harvest ritual,
become one with a million others
who ply this same rite of summer.

There is no boredom here in repetition.
Each pod is its own mystery, its own small world.
And you become the eternal peasant, held
in abounding fascination with living things.
You now become a mere extension
of something you sense but can not fully know:
why this ritual courses small, almost imperceptible
tremors through the nerves and sinews of the arm
to warm the thumb and fingers with old messages.
You lapse into the easy movement of the hands
with a satisfaction that lies just below
the skin of consciousness like tiny emeralds
singing their green notes in mid-summer dance.
In the coolness of early morning you turn
the seasons between your thumb and fingers
and hold the rain in your hands.

KNIVES AND FISH

The old Swampy Cree in the filleting shed
watches our slow butchery of fish
and finally says to us,
Here, I show you howta fillet
d'walleye, dere's nuttin to it atall.

He grasps a plump walleye by the head
pulls a filleting knife from its sheath
makes several quick passes behind the gills
slashes the belly open, slices the side

strips back one side of fish from head to tail
in a flash of fillet, flips the fish over
and flakes the other fillet.

Knives and fish hold no secrets for him.

But we, mouths agape like pike-strikes,
disbelievers at an illusionist's show
stare, try to peel away some small deceit,
something that will explain it all.

See dese bones here? Watch.

He flips the fillet meat-side down
places his thumb on the scales above the bones
slides his knife under the fillet
along the filleting table under the pressure
of his thumb with a soft snick
lifts the fillet, shows us the bones,
a neat sliver lying on the table.

Y'see. Nuttin to it.
Now you do it.

He grins and walks away
wiping his knife blade on his jeans.

EARLY MORNING SUN

1

Two grain elevators
pry the reluctant
sun up from
the horizon
and slowly,
slowly raise it
to their shoulders.

2

I was wrong—again.
There were three
elevators and the sun
was levered up
the sky by two
while the foreman
stood by and watched.

THE AMATEUR GARDENER

The salmon-fleshed begonias have wilted
and died from over-watering, drowned.

Just yesterday he was certain that he
heard them crying out for water.

Their once-proud sockeye blooms are now
a mere soggy memory. To kill with kindness,

he reflects, is every bit as certain as rage,
as he dumps the drowned begonia in the garbage.

Even now he thinks he hears the fern croak
dustily from its pot. He stops his ears.

AMSTERDAM DOG WALKER

Along the canal she came, the young woman
drawn on a spider web of leashes by seven dogs,

seven multi-sized mutts trotting in strange sync
along the canal path in canine unconcern.

When one dog stopped to squat or lift a leg
the other six all automatically dallied;

some sank on haunches, others stood,
but all were trained to treat each stop

as an inalienable right of dogdom. Each
no doubt having its turn to pick and choose

the spot to sniff or snuffle. And the woman
strolled behind, silent and content, holding

the reins of this peculiar everyday procession;
leader or follower, she was vital to the group.

Long after they had passed and disappeared beyond
the canal's curving course, it occurred to me:

it was a silent entourage. Not one yip or yap,
nor growl nor grumble; not one word of admonition

or impatience from her who walked behind. Silent
and uncanny, this promenade of woman and dogs

who knew each other's needs, had made this stroll
so often now there was no need for words,

except the subtle, silent language of the links
of living leash that bound them each to each.

Andrew Suknaski

OVERLAND TO THE SOUTHERN PLAIN

1. henry kelsey arriving at indian village on carrot river

that young whiteman
he funny man say our country belong to his people
this strange medicine
he stand barehead
shout something to wind and river
in his language—our men talk
one man say . . . *this big medicine*
he big medicine

2. kelsey leaving deering's point

that summer the chief of the stones
provided me with several men to protect and lead me
and i was grateful—
for a while we paddled down the great river
and then continued our journey on foot leaving
the forests behind as the land flattened
we lived on small game and often ate berries
whenever we found trees heavy with fruit

at times we saw small herds of buffalo
and once shot one
when it rained for several days—we slowly cooked
big chunks of meat on a skinned branch
we turned over a campfire—

the sweet and coarse soft meat was something to remember
in our hardships
as we journied often hungry till one of us
shot another partridge

finally we reach hills rising above the plain
my indian companions said eagles built nests there
and we camped there for several days and rested—
we feasted on berries and a couple geese
one of us had shot
finally we journied west a few more days and began
the long walk back
to where we had left our canoes
for it was late summer

when we returned to the village just after the first frost
i cut two straight trees and skinned them
and tied them together—
i then raised the cross on that high place
where i had claimed the country of good report
calling the place *deering's point* to honour the man
and carved the following text:
july the 10th 1690 sir edward deering

3. the myth

we watch him put up cross
we thought
this man come so long way to do this
learn our language
live like us
this place be big medicine
he talk peace to naywatamee poets and nayhaythaways
this man this cross big medicine
cross so white on
blue sky

LOVE WITHIN SHADOWS

as a girl lies in the sun
near larches—
her eyes closed
beneath a wave of black hair
on the shore
of her white face
i silently move between her
and the boiling planet
that casts my shadow
like a japanese brushstroke
across her whiteness

and touching her body
this way   suddenly
turns my blood into frost
because i become part
of a mystery
i cannot control or understand

i only know each step
makes the shadow move
along her arm
till i stop
when the shadow
steals the warmth from her face—
i turn my head sideways
and always
the shadow obeys
(the silhouette of my face
touches the edge
of her face)

THE ROBSON STREET WAITRESS

she is the beautiful untouchable
lady
all day
she serves coffee
wipes tables
serves coffee
wipes tables
makes change for the unemployed
men who never have the right change
so they can watch her eyes
while she counts the change
(the moment
the traffic sounds
& the city's day drone
suspended
in their hearts
like a watch an old man carries for weeks
before remembering to wind it)

JIMMY HOY'S PLACE

gee clyz
all time slem ting hoy would say
when he got mad at some obnoxious drunk
stirring hell in the cafe

all time takkie to much
makkie trouble sunna bitch
wadda hell madder wid you?

gee clyz hoy would mutter and scold the man
would shake his small grey head and disappear into
the smoky kitchen to scramble some eggs for the drunk

gee clyz
all time slem ting something would whisper
in the back of hoy's mind
as he sat and smoked his pipe through the long afternoons
in the empty cafe
maybe immersed in a dream where the years became centuries till
a child's coin rapped on the scratched counter
drew hoy from his dream

hoy's early history is uncertain
though some speak of a time when he first arrived at
the old post and built a small cafe and livery stable
and how drunk halfbreeds often rode into the hamlet
to lift hoy onto a table and make him dance
as they shot up the floor

when the railroad came through
and the hamlet was moved five miles north
hoy built a big new cafe complete with false front
the text reading:
HOTEL
wood mountain cafe & confectionery

back in the thirties
hoy threw hank snow out for creating a disturbance
snow had hopped off a freight
thinking a song might rustle up some food in hoy's place—
seems hoy was a bit thin himself and the song nothing new
so he escorted snow to the door
saying: *gee clyz*
all time slem ting

hoy's place was where men drank coffee and told stories
like the one about the time charlie bloiun handled
the village's only holdup
how a killdeer cowboy saw one western too many
and thought he might rob bloiun's store—
following an afternoon of beer in the west central

the man got his shotgun and tied a hanky around his face
and entered the store
while old bloiun counted his money
and whispered: *stickum up*
bloiun briefly pausing to look over his glasses
long enough to say: *pete—you better put that gun down*
before you hurt yourself
and then continued his counting while pete crept out
somewhat embarrassed

hoy's place was where in boyhood one came to know death
when men ceased joking
as someone arrived with first news of men like the jealous agent
from another town—
how he imagined a lover for his beautiful faithful wife
until one day he left a note on the grain scales
saying: *i think it'll be better this way for all of us*
and then walked his .22 behind the elevator
to perform what some believe is the most creative act

hoy's icecream and chinese calendar girls were something to dream
  about
on hot july days of summerfallowing
were something to remember as one woke falling
against the twisted wheel of lovenzanna's tractor
george tonita bought at the auction sale
following the funeral

hoy's place was where we waited on friday mailnights
to glimpse the train's first black smoke beyond the snowfence—
as kids we were fascinated by the engineers and the brakemen
while hoy brought out their steaks and mashed potatoes—
the way they flattened mashed potatoes into thin layers
squared off like dominoes fascinated us
while we searched their eyes for the glow of distant cities
till hoy came saying: *leddem eat—go outside and play*
gee clyz
all time slem ting

KOONOHPLE

for myrna kostash

mother enjoying some tea
and remembering how they grew koonohple back in galicia
tells of baba karasinski planting the precious round seeds
in the spring
and how she later coddled the young green leaves
the male and female plants growing side by side
from a single seed
baba wanting only the best always weeded out the male
so the female could grow tall and strong
there was never any difficulty telling them apart
though the male plants grew first
the females always flourished taller in the end
"why bother with the runts" baba must have thought
"they're only like some geedo . . . an obedient shadow of baba"
she probably assumed that in one's garden at least
things could be perfect
and anyway it was the female who bore all the seeds
she could survive alone

when the crop was ready
baba and geedo would harvest it with sickles
and tie small bundles
later buried in a muddy trench near a creek
where they were left to rot for one week before being dug up
and taken to the creek to rinse
finally koonohple were hung on a fence to dry
and a few days later geedo battered them with a flail
till only the strong hemp thread within the stalks remained
then baba's final delicate work began
using a huge piece of circular wood with many spikes
she would comb and comb the threads
until they became almost as fine as gossamer
then on winter nights baba and other women
got together with their bundles of combed koonohple

to tell stories while they spun by hand
spun every bundle into fine thread wound onto big wooden spools
they called "vahrahtmoos"
and mother says
their arms and hands were their spinning wheels
the thread was dyed with beet plum or carrot juice
and woven into cloth becoming
table cloths towels curtains
and clothes for a whole family

fascinated i ask mother
"what did you do with the seeds leaves and stems
after you flailed koonohple?"
mother sipping her sweet tea slowly remembers
"vee kept seeds fhorr nex yearr
an throw strrah to dha peegz . . .
dhey vaz shure like dhat sthoff"
i ask if she grew koonohple on the farm
she smiles
"shomtimes . . . ohnly leedly bit fhorr burds
i gif dhem seeds in veenterr
oh dhey shurr like dhem . . . sing soh nice"
she tells how in the old country
geedo used to press oil from koonohple seeds
and she wistfully recalls how good it was on salads
a bit of chopped homegrown onion and sliced cucumber
a tad of pepper and salt
"smell soh ghoot . . . dhat oil
vit leedly veenyeeger
nhoting else now *soh* ghood"

smiling i ask mother
"you know what koonohple are mom?"
as she eyes me suspiciously
i tell her
"grass mom 'trahvah' that's the stuff the kids smoke mom"
she lifts her braided fingers high above her head

rolls her eyes heavenward
and exclaims
"oooh my God . . . marryyohnah! dhat's be marryyohnah?"
and now that i mention to mother
how the kids often grow their own hiding it with corn stalks
she slowly remembers how her father
grew his illegal tobacco at the turn of the century
and hid it at the centre of his koonohple crop
that always grew taller all around
she remembers that when the first world war came
tobacco was scarce everywhere in the old country
and geedos suffering withdrawal beat their babas
the old women scuttling to neighbours everywhere
to beg for a bit of tobacco
geedos tried bulrushes and nettles and simply anything
and mother recalls how her grandfather silent as granite
in his corner of the living room
was often lost in a cloud of rising smoke
like a chimney on a cold windless winter morning
baba coughing and chiding geedo
"dgeetko . . . vahryatstvo!
ahbeh tehbeh shlock trahfogh!"
geedo always mumbling between well spaced blissful eternities
and keeping his secret
"fynoo baba . . . fynoo . . . fchoh budeh yak zohlotoh
'beautiful old woman
beautiful . . . everything will be like gold' "

LETTERS BETWEEN TWO PRAIRIE FRIENDS

for j.n.

dear john
 i'm sendin you a contact print
from some photographs found in the album
of an 80 year old widow
my mother shared a house with her
a few winters in assiniboia
told me about her recent fall
spoke of kneelin among scattered
japanese oranges down in the cellar

 'lohrra . . . lohrra
 how deed you get herre lohrra?'

mother cradled the frail small woman
like a child in her arms
tried to rock her awake
         anyway
these photos john i donno
donno why i send em
wonder if you've ever seen em
think it's mostly something to do
with the bottom of stairways
where our lives cross
         anyway the story is
your mother an laura taught at tolstoi
manitoba 1916
their school house was called *chervona*
'the red one'
they shared a thatched roof teacherage
an after they went their separate ways
they always wrote letters
         i remember
the old widow sayin that last time

'when she married
an had her first son
she sent me this photograph
she sometimes wrote
about those years
often nothing   but bread
potatoes an tea
on the table'

that one photograph   john
your mother   a beautiful young
woman then   hair combed   straight an simple
a single lock   covering her right eye
an curving down   to meet smile
forever there   over her son
sleeping in the carriage
where one can almost smell   the lilac hedge
bordering the crunch   of gravel walk
and the long dress she wears
brightening   those black shoes
that mirror the sky
                    anyway   john
i'm sendin you this print
an keepin one for myself
pinned directly   above a family photo
me standin against the lilacs
on my sixth birthday   before we all left
the farm an father   for good
                              i send you these
prairie icons   for the possible
poem   they may unlock

take care,
suknatskyj

dear andrei

never before have i seen a picture of my mother
at that age   i loved her
but we couldn't talk
our family never did
she was a beautiful woman
who lived a very difficult life
i think i'm about ready to   you'll
have to write the poem
i can't

j.

LEAVING HOME AGAIN

leaving home again
suknatskyj knows
it will not be easy
in the darkening avenue
of memory
is fully aware
there'll be no
absolute forgetting
that thursday night
burning grass
in the church yard
that evening
of good intentions
or wakening
from deep sleep
on the sofa
the whole living room
glowing
red

his terrified mother
framed
by the doorway
struggling
for breath

'the choorrch
the choorrch eez burrnin
poorr . . . churrch'

never will suknatskyj forget
the vaulting
pyramidal flames
his heart rising on
bitter tide
people gathering
to stand helpless

the schoolchildren
at recess
ringing the grey bell
with small stones
flung from the road

suknatskyj saying
goodbye
to his mother
who does not
face him

only stretches out
her left hand

'tek dhis lohf   easterr brread
myte you be get   hahgrry
vehrr you   goink'

suknatskyj
on a northbound
bus
where the dark
window
mirrors
nothing
moving alone
in thoughts
of home
and sleep

REGISTRATION OF DEATH / CANADA: PROVINCE OF SASKATCHEWAN

to the memory of peter suknatskyj

. . . on the margins
of all things

I. Name of Deceased in full
If an unnamed child give surname preceded by 'unnamed'. *Died unnamed*

to hear the cock crow
to be gone
the third day
before
naming
by water

to not bear
the chosen name

2. Date of death. *26* day of *Sept.* 1922

. . . on the margins
of all things

6. Place of Death
If outside the
limits of a city, *32 · 4 · 2 · W3*
town or village,
give sec., tp.
and rge.

to lie under
mantling darkness
like a sin marked
by the nameless
stone
in the NE corner
of a cemetery
in the game
preserve
where whitetail deer
descend
the hills
spring to fall
heads angled
under barbed wire
to graze
the tall green
grass

Remark:
(For Registrar
only) *Child reported very frail at birth and*
died suddenly on 3rd day.

to be discovered
in the charred
records
flung by the new
storekeeper
into
the nuisance grounds
on the margins
of all things
lost

TO WHOM IT MAY CONCERN / RE: MISS EVE SUKNATSKYJ, AGE 29

13th april friday good it's not a
how weeks many shock since electricity now
long treatment passed my through brain
they how will be it form can till I
than more a day sentences two?

November 27, 1958

Above mentioned patient was seen for the first time on Oct. 24, 1958, at the psychiatric O.P.D. of the St. Boniface Hospital.

She appeared unclean, untidy, apparently unable to look after herself. Although she was fairly co-operative she refused to be hospitalized for 'multiple sclerosis,' in 1956.

saturday bells winnipeg of them loved i use to
who wonder lives now in room that to left top at
of stairway north kildonan house that
sister pauline to walked st boniface daily
from hospital 40 blocks stolen with food for me
more 40 blocks to back walk that winter . . .
in the end did why i never that door open?
made me what cruel so when her loved i most?
food by left door cold she and often crying
sitting few moments that stairway on to
warm up before home going . . . write in her
as always daily diary

> *1957 Jan 6th*
> *Today my thoughts fly back*
> *to when I was a little girl*
> *when we celebrated Dad's wilia.*
> *How time does change things.*
> *Tonight he sits alone on the farm*
> *with no one to carole to him,*
> *or even to sit with him.*

> With the help of Social Service and Welfare Departments, patient was coaxed to come in on Nov. 6, 1958. Her neurological findings displayed ataxic nystagmus, 4 limb pyramidal tract syndrome, moderate cerebellar disease, sl. intention tremor and slow scanning speech. Mentally she was about the same as on Oct. 24th, when seen at the O.P.D. she was well oriented, her memory seemed unaffected although occasionally she seemed incredible. There was no psychotic symptom. Her mood was somewhat flattened. At times she giggled and behaved in a silly way. Generally she displayed some euphoria.

why do they treat us this way? why do we have to
leave these crumbling walls, and
go out into the city on week days, to scrub and
polish floors for prominent doctors—all for
nothing? and here . . . why can these sane young
men, who are supposed to be caring for us, take us
anytime they wish? and do whatever they please.
i remember that day, them behind the divider—
their groans, and her young muffled voice. did
they really believe, they could erase it from
her memory with electricity the next day? today,
i must write a letter.

dear mom & andrei

it's so lonely in here. it's so long since
anyone has come to see me. they don't give us
very much to eat in here. metro, could you
please send me a few apples and oranges?
and maybe a few chocolate bars. my favourite
bar was always cuban lunch.

love,
eve

p.s. mom, please pray for me. pray i will
get better.

Patient's greatest problem was her addiction to Equanil and her wish to have a job. She was discharged on Nov. 20th, 1958, placed on Sparine and promised to appear regularly at the O.P.D.

After a few days however, it was reported by the Social Services Department that patient apparently had slipped back into her habit and was unable to look after herself.

as a small girl, my life began shelling peas from the garden
on the farm. now, it ends shelling peas again. me seated
on the hard green chair. these hands once held the needle
or a patient's wrist. my face once resembling a beautiful
serene nun. my face now like some escarpment crumbling
into a river. joy now the light in the eyes of the baby
crawling between thin feet of the young girl who helps
me shell these chrisly peas. the baby was born here last
christmas eve.

Since she is not co-operative, it is necessary
to institutionalize this patient.

Yours truly,

Wolfgang Helm, M.D.
Assistant Resident
in Psychiatry

it ends with this. hydroemiclysis. i am no longer fed
intravenously. long needles inserted
directly into me—my world now,
pure oxygen, crystal memory, a tent. all sounds
and voices still there, clear as the sharp ring
of a coin falling on stone.

'eve, can you hear me now?
mom took the greyhound from
moose jaw last night.
the village took up a collection
for the fare. she's coming
to see you . . . eve'

of course i can hear you sister. but how can i tell you now

MANHATTAN BORSCHT

noonhour suknatskyj
a mouth upon him
for hot soup
suknatskyj fawning
over the menu

'nah honey!
we got nah clamcahdeh tahday
jis soupahdahday honey . . . '

'well wahddabout these three soups here?
chicken noodle
split pea
an this here borshch?
kin i have some borshch?'

'well we dowen really call thadda soup honeh!'

'tzokay okay with me
i'll have some'

an eternity later
manhattan borshch arrives
a scoop
of sour cream
with a generous handful of
finely chopped
beets floating around
. . . suspiciously
no suggestive steam wafting up
to commingle
deliciously
with hint
of dill

suknatskyj
uneasily stirs it all
muses
where
are my broad beans
tasting of prairie earth?

stirs that dollop
of sour cream
becoming a dozen
hopeless islands
something
reminiscent of ice floes
in a sea
of thin
raspberry juice!

flatfaced suknatskyj
takes a tentative spoonful
to tease
tastebuds
'UGH!
ICECOLD!
MANHATTAN
BORSHCH!'

cornercafé mamma
casually explaining
'well honeh
maybe some *jewish* place
heats it up
bahddats the way we shevvit heeh . . . honeh!
ICECOLD!
reeefrrrehshin! onna hot
new yok day'

Anne Szumigalski

ANGELS

have you noticed
how they roost in trees?
not like birds
their wings fold the other way

my mother, whose eyes are clouding
gets up early to shoo them
out of her pippin tree
afraid they will let go their droppings
over the lovely olive
of the runnelled bark

she keeps a broom by the door
brushes them from the branches
not too gently
go and lay eggs she admonishes

they clamber down
jump clumsily to the wet ground
while she makes clucking noises
to encourage them to the nest

does not notice how they
bow down low before her anger
each lifting a cold and rosy hand
from beneath the white feathers
raising it in greeting
blessing her and the air
as they back away into the mist

THE ARRANGEMENT

she's arranging irises in a polished brass vase as elegant and narrow-shouldered as herself *made from a bombcase* she explains to the tall blue flags stiff as april that will not obey her arthritic fingers *1916* she adds softening the effect with a spray of ferny leaves

bombs falling on london all around the town whistling down from silvery zeppelins which nose about in the sky huge docile fish swimming in the upper air

she stalks naked through the dark rooms watching her reflection flicker in grey mirrors soft thin body, pale legs, wiry red hair resting uneasily on white shoulders and freckled arms she peers closer examines the small uneven face the emphatic mouth the smallpox scar between the foxy brows

this is the first time she has ever been alone in the forest-hill house where she was born

if ever she was born for there's no record of any such birth of any such person as herself, none she found that out at her wedding five months ago *you are marrying nobody* and she rests her fingers lightly on the two stars on william's epaulette then leans forward and kisses him on the mouth she can feel that her warm lips shock him for he's younger and much shyer than she is *bill my will* she whispers again to the dark house this lonely night *can you survive all this? can I?*

for she carries in her velvet belly a weight lighter than a burr a kernel from which a red-haired child may grow

now she's in the cool garden hugging her thin arms round her fine nakedness chalkwhite roses bloom in their beds their stems and thorns black as blood   one open flower stares up at her with the pinched face of an infant about to cry

the earth shrieks   cracks apart   rumbles   shakes shakes   and trembles to a stop

fish has laid his tumble of eggs among the pavements and the houses   the school crumples   the churchtower falls into the park   the walls of the prison break open and men rush out thanking the fishgod for their deliverance almost at once they turn into muddy soldiers grumbling and joking about the war, the mud, wet feet, rats and the rotten bitter war

she lies flat in the roses covered with plaster dust from next door thorns clawing at her chin and her breasts the cocklebur little nut moves within her parts from its seedcase and drops from her to the earth followed by a narrow warm trickle

she scratches among the roses as a cat might then buries the tiny thing without a tear stands up dizzy lighter by the weight of a handful of leaves

in the house she draws the heavy curtain so close that not a chink parts them then lights a candle and flings herself onto the wide bed   a small empty space aches within her, aches coldly through her sleep which lasts long into the next day

downstairs in the back kitchen where the window
is broken and the door swings loose on its hinges
the small debris of the city has been sifting into
the house all night a layer of fine particles covers
the sink and the green glass flower-holders by
morning the shelf and the vases that stand there
—blue raku, enamelled chinoiserie, silver beaten
thin as steam—are greyed with a layer of fine
detritus which might be the dust of a century

SHRAPNEL

shrapnel has torn the man's ribs apart
there is a shabby wound in his breast
his mouth opens innocently upon a cry

he wants to curse his enemies but cannot
for he sees them as striplings lying in the grass
each with a girl beneath him
the long grass full of clover and fieldherbs
waves gently in the heat
the men get up from the women
and buckle on their belts
the women just lie there looking up at the thundery sky
we are wounded with joy they tell each other
we are happy happy happy

the soldier sees this he hears all this
as he lies there asking the earth
is this my final place my own place
he glances upwards to where
the tops of the trees almost meet
there is just a small patch of empty sky showing
it must be spring for a bird with a straw in its beak
swoops down to a low bough he tries to think

of the name of the bird
he tries to think of his own name
the name of his son who has learned to speak already
so his wife writes   he has seen the child only once
and that was more than a year ago

he tries to remember the colour of his wife's eyes
he sees only her frailty those little narrow birdbones
beneath the soft flesh
he wishes she was another woman
one easier to abandon   one calm and robust
with a wide smooth brow

but who could forget that pitiful teat
in the child's mouth
the curious maze of blue milkveins whose pattern
he traces in the dirt   his hand touches a broken brick
here was a house   now he remembers the collapse
of its walls

he licks his lips tasting for brickdust
he counts his strong teeth with his tongue
they are all there unchipped   he hears the bland
voice of the dentist telling him he has perfect bite

he shuts his eyes against the light but it shines on
through rosy lids which are the same colour exactly
as his wife's secret he wants to part her legs
and touch her glistening vermillion lining
now at last he understands
why he loves the bodies of women
more than the bodies of men   for pale skin covers
a man all over and only a wound can show his lining

carefully he passes his hands over his body
buttoned into its tunic of stiff drab wool
until he finds the hole in his chest
he thrusts in his fist to staunch the blood

a pulse beats close to his folded fingers
it is insistent and strong
it is pushing him away from himself

THE BEES

you speak in a dry voice of the sunburnt skin on the face of the woman who tells through a mouthful of grit of an unpainted house scoured by the sun where she stands on an old chair with a thin rag in her hand trying to clean the window where dirt has lodged in the corners of the frame

she tells of when you were a boy lying faceup in a field of many-coloured clover set upon by bees their humm humm bumblebees groundbees purring in their furry bodies you see them huge as cats leaping from the clover flowers and chasing you down the gravel road through a wire fence and into a field of tall green wheat where you crouch breathless with your hands around the back of your neck trying to ward off those darts from piercing the delicate flesh behind your earlobes

the hum grows louder and louder it comes from overhead where one lazy plane is flying and now the earth tilts so that the sky is below you are falling into a pit of sky deeper than the slough deeper than the well

slowly through space you fall for more than a month you name the days as you fall you write the names with a white pencil of smoke on the walls of the sky on the fourth sunday you see that at last you are approaching the plane a silver insect not at all like a bee it is tin like a christmas present its edges sharp as a toy car hood

after dinner you play in the yard with your new toy you don't need winter boots because there is no snow *this is a black christmas* your mother explains *it is dark all over there is a war on we must pray for peace* and she ties her new red kerchief very tight under her chin

outside it is stony cold the pebbles under your feet are sharp you can see the pointed stars they sting your eyes with their light the yard is silvery not black you throw the tin plane up it falls into the trough where a foal is drinking there is ice on the foal's lip

humm humm humm the airplane flies through the night the passengers are singing as they fly *you are younger than you were in the summer* they sing *you are getting younger all the time soon you will shrink down to a baby small enough to get back into your mother you will ride inside her all winter you will hear the squelch of the floor-mop you will hear the squeak of the cloth as you try to clean the corners of the window*

while you were away while you were off in the sky the woman and the house have crumbled and blown away now there is just one wall left standing just one window with no glass through it you can see the prairie and far away the crumpled riverbed under the window stands an old chair with a rung missing and a stained cooking pot full of rain where a bumblebee is collecting water for her family, they live in a hole in the ground

and dryly you explain to your child how the sun
is really an image of our idea of the sun just as
the prairie is a reflection of our need for flatness
consider you tell him *the clever dance of the bee*
which is in the exact shape of her idea of distance

LOOKING FOR UNCLE TICH IN THE WAR CEMETERY

o tenderness of heaven rain down on army tombstones
this is the song the band plays while under the sun
spiders are crawling up hot marble   a time to
crawl up   a time to swing down again   a time
to shrivel leaving the next generation to get to the
top and over

a kiosk contains the book which contains the names
of the fallen a perfect record of those boxfuls of
bones brittle under caved-in coffin lids under stony
soil and lilac sky   this is the burrowing beetles'
world that the spider knows nothing of

some died with all their flesh on, some with both
eyelids to close over both eyes our young guide has
the air of a lover on a postcard smarmed-down hair
forgetmenot eyes   a bird flies through the picture
is that a hawk you ask nervously *a falcon* he replies
without master or jess

when we tell of our uncle here since 1916 not once
disturbed by visitors it takes his breath away, *no one*
here of that name he sighs and closes the book later
we find the little soldier under an alias of his
rascally boyhood

tomorrow this place will be closed for the season
shed padlocked, gates barred   the marching band
will sit on the grass polishing brass instruments with
khaki rags   at a signal each man will get to his
feet preparing his lips for the last blow

while the industrious spider lays her eggs in the
body of a beetle strayed into the light

ON SINGLENESS

Today I've become for the first time a lonely woman,
A lonely woman in a woollen skirt and shawl

Moving heavily from one room to another,
Back and forth from the bedroom to the kitchen,

From the kitchen to the storeroom.
I've become someone deciding what to do next,

While the daylight lasts;
What to do next

While the oil lasts for the lamp,
The logs for the stove.

In the crock a half-loaf, in the cupboard/cheese
Wrapped in its vinegared muslin,

Two tins of corned beef on the shelf,
In the back of the store five jars

Of lakefish, two of riverfish, berries and
Berries, then mushrooms:

Twenty jars pickled and eleven jars dried,
A small sack of wheat, when opened
Smells softly of mould,

And salt in a block like cattle salt.

I count everything over and over.
I wipe the tops of the jars

I murmur *that's all, that's all.*
I have become an old woman

With cold hands counting jars.
That's all, that's all.

And later out with the maul
To split wood, the last of the wood

That we sawed in the last of the summer.
The block rings like a stone struck.

Shivers of snow fall from the branches.
Above me the usual raven sits in the naked tree,

Croaking his dry claim to my answer.
My dark companion I tell him,

After the logs are split, after the kindling
Is chopped into white slivers,

I shall come with my chipped enamel dishpan
And gather clean snow,

Being careful to keep away from
The bird tracks, the mouse seed,
The rabbit scat.

ON THE SUN

Journeys are all circular.
There's someone at the centre holding

The swung pail from which no water falls.
There's someone holding

The lunging rope, someone blindfold
In the middle of the game.

So round and round
Round and round you go,

The whole earth round.

O pony on the beaten lunging track
Do you imagine you're making a new claim

To earth's old journey?

Ah, Sun-flower weary of time,
Who counteth the steps of the sun;
Seeking after that sweet golden clime,
Where the traveller's journey is done. (WM BLAKE)

You are the one who moves on his axis,
Turning that cheek, this cheek
To the warmth of the sun.

Round and round on the twisted neck
Of a green stem
The corolla with its ray florets

Swinging to the lights of sunrise
Of sunset.

Never deceive such a flower,
Advises the old herbalist

With lanterns or torches for in five days
It will twist its head off.

HALINKA

It is right, they say, to bury a stillborn child with a mirror on the pillow beside her. That way, at the resurrection, when she opens her eyes for the first time, she will see her face and recognize herself.

But that's not for you, little daughter, little flaccid creature. For you, there never was such a thing as a face. There were hands and fingers, curled feet with curled toes. There was a heart in your chest, red and whole as a candy, and a white iris growing in the place of your understanding.

THE FLIGHT

of angels: the sough of air through their feathers: the fanatic beat of their pinions: the celestial honking of their song. Either they have just passed over or they are about to darken the morning with the wings of their thousand formations, each with the head of Azrael at the arrow's point. Their necks outstretched, they rush past the clouds like geese in autumn, like swans in the spring.

But these do not travel to the North or to the South. Westward only they circle the planet, scooping up this one and that one. Our souls that leap from the body are gathered to them, to nestle in white down. As lice on pelicans, as mites on cranes, we infest the holy pink skin of angels.

THE BOY AT THE UPSTAIRS WINDOW WITH HIS HEAD IN HIS HANDS

it is heavy as a stone he tells himself like any rock in the field of rocks on grandfather's farm where boulders are born out of the prairie every spring if these are the heads of huge stone infants where are the bodies to follow narrow from shoulder to toes after the round agony of the head or could they be ancient skulls that the earth gives up a thousand years after their burial what with the rain and the wind something must surely come to light in the end for this is in many ways the field of jesus the place where he decided to make an end of his journey he who had travelled as far as india and back he who has been seen in every city in the world at one time or another just walking around stirring up trouble many times thrown into jail for disturbing the peace of such places as this where the bones of the earth break up and are carried away by farmers who make piles of them in the corners of every field and dear are these rockpiles to the child they are his mountains and ramparts and sometimes he sees brilliant snakes slithering in the cracks the rocks also are of every colour and grandfather says if you split one of these suckers you could find a coiled seashell or a perfect fern or perhaps just a hollow place the boy understands that this hollow is the very same secret room where he lives always alone tracing the mysterious maps on the walls with a wetted finger trying to find how to get away from cartoons of rabbits and cats in heroes' hats to where fair ladies are advertising the subtle gifts of the mind

Jon Whyte

MAGOT PIE

for Buck Kerr

Only his head, nape, cape, part of his back
are black;
the lizard black of the rest of him,
the chevrons on his wings, is black-blue,
an iridescent hue
we might confuse
with the black-green hues
of his tight-wire walker's balance-pole tail feathers
which wobble like wigwags when he lights
on a limb,
the monad Harlequin motleyed in days and nights.

(Better to refer to it as «she»
than «he,»
the «maggoty-pie» or «Margaret»
who, like «Phylypp sparrow,» «Jenny wren,»
«Tom tit,» Redbreast «Robyn,»
was named and known
by given name alone,
not by *pica pica*, or «pie,» but «Margot,» «Madge,»
more like a raucous ululation
of knife whet,
sharpening blade in carrion anticipation?)

«For brigandage and rapine» the pie
            relies
upon a cloistered quiet until
the «unscrupulous roysterer» falls,
        fans his spread spades, stalls,
        «and has no shame»
in a losing game
«showing its terror and calling on the whole world
to witness the unprecedented
            outrage.» Ill
luck in seeing him is by three times spitting averted.

In Scotland, magpies' flying by a
            «wind-eye»
means death is near; spotted on a walk,
«one's sorrow, two's mirth, three's a wedding,
        four's a birth,» proceeding
        «seven's heaven,
eight is hell, and nine's
the devil his ane sel'.» Most unlucky, to see
nine Sumi-quick calligraphic strokes
            in «soft-talk»
of penguins, tuxedos, the jewellery of rich folks.

The ideograms they flash in Quink
            methinks
are not concerned with nuns or prelates,
but mayhap with undertaker or
        barrister, solicitor,
        or penmanship
shot straight from the hip
«as western as a coyote, a cayuse, or a
coulee»; yet glinted with Chinese white,
            dissipate
their green-blue blackness in an auroral night.

Can one discern messages they write
            in bright
cursive calligraphy, like Franz Kline's
dash? Or Buck Kerr's shaded winter sun
        scattered in precision
        on a blank sheet
within print black neat-
ness which is the preened sheen of a pair, a tidings
of «Madges,» the prisms of pinions
            and the signs
to be read upon snow's dominions?

«The dinosaurs are not extinct; they
            became
the birds.» Yearned, leaning on a branch, head
stretched forward, tail feathers erect, ribald
        in rancour, the piebald
        gazette squawking
sounds like the talking
of a pair of pies in badinage arguing
about their saurian origin,
            how they bred
themselves, how evolved their awkwardness and being.

MORE OR LESS

Of negative capability, I can remember nothing
Of the two pillars of Hercules I can remember one
and of the two eyes of Greece I recall one
one of the two moons of Mars, two of the three basic chords, two of
            the three musketeers (and of the four musketeers, three,
            and of them, of course, only two)
two of the three basic types of triangle;
I can jog my mind for two of the three types of the ten mysteries
            (of the ten mysteries, twenty mysteries, thirty mysteries,
            none)

two of the three f's, all three of the r's, of the three tongues two
and three of the primary colours additive, one of the primaries subtractive,
or as many as I can recall of the two coordinate axes
I can recall three of the four humours, three of the four states of matter,
three of the four horsemen of the Apocalypse, two of the
three graces,
one less than there were teams in the NHL
and now I don't know how many teams there are in the NHL
three of the four freedoms, three of the four p's
two of the three ruling gods of the ancients
three of Eliot's *Four Quartets* and some of the several *Versions of Pastoral*
four of the five Platonic solids,
five of the wives of Henry the Eighth (and, of course, all eight of
the Henry's)
one less than there are categories of «Seven Wonders of . . . »
or just as many dwarves' names when I'm trying to fall asleep
six of the seven basic plots, six of the seven deadly sins, six of the
seven cardinal virtues, six of the *Seven Types of Ambiguity*,
six of the seven days of creation, six of the seven seas,
six of the wonders of the ancient world, all of the seven
days of the week
ten of the members of the Group of Seven
putting me at least one over the eight
and . . . now let me see, where was I?
two of the three wise men, unless they come from Quebec,
three of the parts of the *Alexandria Quartet*, ditto *The Golden Notebook*
all of the four suits
four of the «Five Nations,» five of the «Six Nations» (of which there
were two so-called, but I don't know about the other one
right now)
six of the seven champions, six of the seven gifts of the spirit, gods
of luck, two of the trivium, three of the quadrivium—which
means five of the seven liberal arts, six of the seven senses
six of the works of mercy, and none of the *Seven Pillars
of Wisdom*
all of Santa's seven reindeer
but only seven of the parts of speech

eight of the nine muses
until by the nine gods, I can swear by eight
nine of the ten provincial capitals, eight of the nine hierarchies of angels
and eight of the nine hierarchies of devils
only nine of the Ten Commandments, which has been known to get me
into trouble
eleven of the «Twelve Days of Christmas,» all of the twelve months,
nine of the Ten Peaks
all of the twenty-six letters, the thirty-two points of a compass, five of
the thirty-six basic dramatic situations, nine of the planets
unless there be more, five of the parts of Kenneth Burke's
pentad
somewhere around forty of the one hundred and four plus elements
. . . and there's one more I know I can't remember all of
but it escapes me right now what it is

RUDDY AND MASKED DUCKS

from The Ducks Geese and Swans of North America *by Francis H. Kortright Toronto, published by the Stackpole Company, Harrisburg, Pennsylvania and Wildlife Management Institute, Washington D.C.*

RUDDY AND MASKED DUCKS
Subfamily *Erismaturinae*
(*Oxyurinae,* of Peters)

Ruddy Duck
Erismatura jamaicensis rubida
(*Oxyura jamaicensis rubida,* of Peters)

SCIENTIFIC NAME
Erismatura from Greek, *ereisma*, meaning a stay or prop,
and *oura*, meaning a tail (referring to the stiffened tail);
jamaicensis, Latinised form, meaning of or pertaining to
Jamaica (whence this bird was originally described as the

Jamaica Shoveller, in 1785); *rubida*, Latin, meaning ruddy; *Oxyura*, from Greek *oxy*, meaning sharp, and *oura*, meaning a tail.

COLLOQUIAL NAMES
In general use: Butterball; ruddy.
In local use: Biddy; blackjack;
blatherskite
(varied to blatherscoot, blatterscoot, bladderscoot);
bluebill; bobbler; booby; booby coot;
bristletail; broadbill; broadbill dipper;
brown duck; brown teal; buck-ruddy; bullneck;
bumblebee-buzzer; bumblebee coot;
butterbowl; butterduck; canard roux (russet duck);
chunk duck;
coot;
creek coot;
dapper; daub duck; deaf duck;
dicky; dinky; dipper; dipper duck; dip-tail diver;
dopper; dumb-bird; dumpling duck; dummy duck; dunbird;
fool duck;
god-damn;
goose teal; goose widgeon; greaser; hard head;
hard-headed broadbill; hard tack; heavy-tailed duck;
hickory head; Johnny Bull; leatherback; leather breeches;
light-wood-knot; little soldier; marteau; mud dipper;
murre; muskrat duck; noddy paddy; paddywack; pantail;
quilltail coot; rook; rudder bird; rudder duck;
salt-water teal; shot pouch; shanty duck; sinker;
sleeper; sleeping booby; sleepy broadbill; sleepy brother;
sleepy coot; sleepy duck; sleepy-head; sleepy-jay;
soldier duck; spatter; spatterer; spiketail; spinetail;
spoonbill; spoon-billed butterball; steelhead; sticktail;
stifftail; stiff-tailed widgeon;
stiffy; stub-and-twist; stub-tail;
tough-head; water-partridge; widgeon; widgeon coot; wiretail.

Masked Duck
Nomonyx dominicus

SCIENTIFIC NAME
Nomonyx, from Greek, *nomos*, meaning law, order, and *onux*, meaning nail, i.e., nail of bill ordinary; *dominicus*, Latinised form, meaning of St. Domingo, an island republic in the West Indies.

COLLOQUIAL NAMES
None in North America

LEARNING THE WORLD SPINS

Learning the world spins, I wondered why
it did not fling us off,
Episode **the older of my brothers having demonstrated**
with the hand-cranked gramophone the nature of
the force by placing aggies on the turntable and easing in the clutch.
(Harold argued from his august eight,
(it was the spinning somehow held us in
(by filling up a bucket almost full
(and twirling while he held it in both hands.
(I thought he demonstrated that the earth was
somehow retroflexive,
(the Earth containing at its core the flaming sun.
(His argument he was the sun
(demonstrably held less water than the bucket.)

Learning the world spins, I hoped it possible
I could be free of it by leaping up,
Epifocus **by leaping high enough to watch the world run**
widdershins while I would land a somewhere else
a league or more away, and thus by leaps and hopes and hops
I'd circumnavigate the globe till I got home.

Elaborate conceits availed themselves
to bolster hoped-for tropes of global travel:
the earnest naïve David Douglas notion we all have had
of coming home from opposite the way we went.

I stationed kids to watch me run away,
although I would not hope for hopping leaps,
private tests having demonstrated—even on the park's big swings—
I lacked the oomph to elevate myself enough to stay aloft
a long enough to let the Earth's enantiodromia reveal itself.
I told them by a periphrastic mumble
I'd circumnavigate the circumgyrate twirling ball of Earth and
—not pausing long enough to explicate my crossing of the oceans—
starting eastward, I would arrive *circumbendibus*
ten minutes later from the western edge of town.
By their circumspective nods they gave their doubts away.

It was elusiveness that led me through the woods
(audacious proof that thrust my stomach up my neck,
(requiring that I swallow all my fears of bears)
and when I had returned they all were gone.
Still I hoped that running broad jumps were a way
that track stars had of leaping high enough
the world slipped out from under them.

The like inquisitive curiosity led me to wonder
where a kid like me could buy a magic carpet;
Epicrisis **since science failed me, I'd resort to arcane arts.**
Mother told me Mrs Round (I'm not making this up;
her name was Elsie Round; it had been Elsie Squayre),
who owned the Odd Craft Shop, might carry them,
in the back room tucked away
behind the racks that held the Thorton W. Burgess books
I had by then read most of
(for I was on to Sinbad, rocs, Ali Baba, and Aladdin;
(and Scheherezade's albeit-bowdlerized stories
fascinated me more than Old Mother West Wind's tales).

After lunch I left at five past one
to stop en route at Mrs Round's
and ask her were I to save my pennies, nickels, dimes
from my allowance,
might I purchase one.
***"I'm awfully sorry, Jonny,"* quoth Mrs Round**
as she peered over her glasses to look me in the eye,
"I'm awfully sorry, but I haven't any flying carpets
"in my stock just now. They are becoming scarce.
"But I will let you know should one come in."

" . . . Should one come in" she'd said.
I scarce believed my luck.
Epiphora **"*How much would just a small one cost?*" I must**
have asked. She wasn't sure,
but not beyond the means of one who really wanted. . . .

I floated on to Miss Brown's classroom,
getting there with just scant seconds before the classes started,
and had to wait till recess to tell the other kids
I had first dibs on Mrs Round's next flying carpet,
having to explain how wonderful a magic carpet was
and what it did
and how it worked.
I think she must have told me, or I'd read,
how difficult they are to manage,
to make the carpet do as it was told
and how I might not get to make it work 'til I was older.
Wise of her to be so cautious.

I must have asked her two or three times more at two-week intervals
if she had heard from Persia or Baghdad.
Epigee **She told me only I should keep on hoping.**
I kept on hoping.
I'd sit cross-legged and my hands upon my knees
in what I thought a pasha fashion ought to be,
turbaning my brow in pasha passion,
sitting on the little carpet in the bedroom

that in its interstitial indigo and blood red pattern
intimated Araby,
and close my eyes
and wish
and wish
and misperceive my silent muscles' spasms
as the tug of mind to what could matter,
and hope to levitate myself and it
'til I should feel the ceiling tap my head.
It never happened.
(Was that the year that Bubby and the Mount-Teen Club
(performed *Aladdin?* Loius Worthington and Ted Stafford
(in a comic camel by the name of Nuphsed? Nuphsed.)
Santa Claus by then had metamorphosed into myth,
But Sammy Ward assured me with a twinkling eye
Epiphenomenon **he'd seen a magic carpet once in India,**
and told me of another thing more wonderful
he'd seen while he was there:

"It were in Bombay.
"in a bazaa' there,
"we 'eared a feller playing flute and follered
"through the mazy alleyz 'til we found 'im
"and zeen him zwaying back and forth and zlowly
"oop the lid from orf 'iz bazket moved,
"and oop it zidled, did 'iz rope
"az though it were a znake alive,
"and 'eld thar in the air, joost like a worm,
"and then 'e put 'iz flute bezide
"and told 'iz lad to climb it, oop the rope;
"which 'e did, egzept 'e 'ezitated at the top
"and zhouted down in 'eathen tongue
" 'e'd go no further.
"Zo the feller took 'iz zord and brandished it,
"and zhure enough 'iz lad went further oop and disappeared.
"It were a mozt myzteriouz thing."

To prove a magic by another magic
did not seem dubious at all.

> ***"Then 'e called 'im to coome back down again,***
> ***"and we 'eared zhouting, 'No! No!'***
> ***"Zo then 'e grips 'iz zord between 'iz teeth***
> ***"and climbz 'iz rope and zhoutz again.***
> ***"We 'ear 'iz lad zhout back.***
> ***"Zo then 'e zwingz 'iz zord oop in the air***
> ***"and all the zhouting oot of air iz zilent***
> ***"Zo 'e climbz back down,***
> ***"picks oop 'iz flute***
> ***"and ztartz to play again.***
> ***"Iz rope beginz to zway and zidle in the air***
> ***"and zlowly fall back down and coil into 'iz bazket;***
> ***"and then 'e takez the lid***
> ***"and plazez it atop 'iz bazket joost like that.***
> ***"Zoodenly we 'eared a zhouting moofled-like***
> ***"and from the bazket ztepz 'iz lad entire again.***
> ***"It were a mozt remarkable event,***
> ***"and I zhould like to zee it 'appen once again***
> ***"to tell me that me eyez 'ad never told me lie."***

His telling was so real it kindled faith.

Sammy was a carpenter from London who affected Yorkshire on occasion but retreated to his Cockney for his tales of Albert and the Lion, or other Ramsbottom recounts.

Were there such magic as he told of,
surely I could find a flying carpet.
In all my delitescent fantasies I read of more vehicular phenomena.

Were Mrs Round not sure
(for she was speaking now of "years" instead of weeks)
I'd find another way.
Now I had heard of "Seven-League Boots"
and they replaced my fading hope

of ever getting Mrs Round to say just when
I might expect my carpet to come in
with the hope the other kids had quite forgotten too
my erstwhile hope of getting one, of owning one,
Epiphonema **with the hope of yet another hope,**
a hoped-for hope of boots
to bear their wearer in one pace full seven leagues.
I knew by then better than to ask my mother once again
where they might be for sale, but asked her, sneakily,
just how far a league might be,
and she supposed it was about as far as Anthracite,
and wondered why I'd want to know a thing like that.

(I've looked it up:
(a league can vary from a distance of 2.42 statute miles
(up to 4.6,
(reckoned usually at somewhere nearabouts 3,
(which means that Mother was nearabout correct.
(How did she know a thing like that?)

McCaffrey's was the place for shoes,
for Dubbin, Black Cat polish, shoe repairs,
for leather straps and laces,
and it smelt of tanners' oak,
of richly warm and acrid odours,
cobblers' thoughts,
Morocco, neat's-foot, tannin, gall, and sumac,
exotic places that McCaffrey's craft had cosened.

I know I knew not quite what I expected:
something like a pair of ammonites
with toes like hops that would unfurl to seek far hills
and tow me somehow swiftly in their lee,
or winklepickers with a self-propelling sole,
or Slinkies fastened to a geta-bridge,
or daddy-long-legs coils to spring like Zoomerangs from out the heels.
But Mr McCaffrey said he didn't know what I was speaking of.

How could I know we do not have to jump to move?

By staying in one place we move in slow and elegant pavannes
as continents raft slowly on the globe,
Epeirogenic **and where we might have been is somewhere else**
and where we are is just the carpet longing
for the tugs and yearns of everything to be somewhere else.

We watch the exoskeletons of sea creatures confetti down,
like ash, like dust, like time itself,
to massive banks of quartzite, settling down, becalming,

Christopher Wiseman

THE DEAF-MUTE CHILDREN

Surprised by the silence I turn.

All seven are deaf and dumb,
their excited moving hands
making the bus behind me
a cage of wild white birds.
Nervous, I light a cigarette.

Off the bus, through the trees,
I run to meet my son,
words booming in my head,
gestures fluttering in the air.

THE SPHINX WASP

Attacking yards ahead
of its thin wire of sound,
it has the blank uneccentric
purpose of a missile.
Twisting and diving
it homes like a Phantom
on a flight deck,
trailing its sting
like an arrester-hook.
Finding one dead
you are surprised
it is not painted metal.

The system is neat.
Stung and paralysed,
the spider is dragged
two feet underground
to a prepared chamber
and arranged.
The eggs are laid
and the ravenous larvae
emerge to a whole world
of warm living meat.
Gorging they grow.
When they crawl out,
wasps,
they take off and search
automatically for spiders.

Once, on a patio
in America's heartland,
I watched the process.
For all its running
the spider had no chance.

And today I think of others,
the small frightened ones
half the world away,
who hear American wings
and feel the sickening
blow from the sky.

Blankly, efficiently,
we are storing up corpses
for our children.

PRAYER FOR MY CHILDREN

There are times in the night when I grieve for them my
children when I almost believe I was wrong to have brought
them here where the rockets rest nervously underground under
the sea where nuclear waste is dumped casually where the
rain turns acid eating the soft globe gently as gently as I
held them once lifting them into soft towels where crazy men
have guns and bombs and faces of hate where the quiet
torturers are always at work asking questions questions
through the screams where the whales and tigers are nearly
gone and I hate it all and know I don't really belong to
their world and don't want to and I know they feel so much
but don't know how to feel in shapes because their world is
all dip and whirl and plunge and noise instead of pattern
which I want and need and they don't think they do because
as children they must reject the shapes of my old longings
my music my books all of us who brought them here and left
them and oh I would raise them high to the huge protecting
moon if I could but the moon is dirty now and space is full
of cameras and weapons and I would I swear it gladly lie on
sacrificial stone and let the knife end me if that would
hold their futures intact shape their raw hopes shelter them
from the eating rain the harpoons of a sour and greedy world
soothe the throb of their longing as they reach out hands
for meaning in all of this for something clean and soft and
gentle that will not hurt for their own quiet shapes to live
in and then in other places minute black sacks of bones lie
eyes still moving waiting the ultimate wait too weak to
reach for anything so can I only pity give money try to be
gentle put words on this paper when it's too little and no
good but far too much to carry and the nights last far too
long and I'm saying save them now and later and I'm saying
keep hope behind their eyes and I'm begging keep hope behind
their eyes behind the softness of their eyes

BARBARIAN REMEMBERS AND LOVES HIS CHILDREN

more and more
these days
old voices and places
turn vacantly
inside his head

he looks forward less

once he had
a kingdom where
the land met the sea
and he ran in it
and shouted at the sea

starfish dripped in his hands

he caught great
dark red crabs
and marvelled
at their slowness

he stared into pools
and was calmly but
sharply reflected

above him contrails
and soft gunfire
in the high clouds
and sometimes bombs fell
near him and his brother
until he thought
his mother would cry
all her life

he found shells
of white by the sea
and silver shells
from a Messerschmitt
he kept them together

his children in the city
should know all of this
he will tell them
when they wake
afraid of all the noises
he will tell them
how he would wait
in the shining air
for the tide to uncover
its small brittle things

but especially
he will tell them
how he waited
most patiently
for his father
in strange blue clothes
to come home

THE QUESTION

long ago
his footprints
were washed
from the sand
at Flamborough

should he
go back
for what he
might see
when the tide
uncovers
the sand

or stay
away
his sleep
each night
breaking
with tides
the salt smell
sweet in
his head
the footprints
young and
arrow-straight
clear in
the sand
at Flamborough?

FLAMBOROUGH HEAD

The heart drains slowly,
Fills again, drains and fills.

Sudden heaves of water
Explore the weakness of soft stone.

I shouldn't come here.
I have been too far away.

It hurts to contain such fullness
And erosion, these long tides

Which rinse the memory.
Yet I have loved this place,

And the draining and filling
Make the chained heart move,

Make time flow strong and dizzy
Through the starved and landlocked mind.

COD FISHING

Cold November nights are best
With the high tide whipped
By a razor wind, the waves
Exploding like shells on the rocks

Like tonight.
The fingers can hardly grip
To put the lugworm on
To control the huge cast

Over the seaweed and rocks
Eighty yards with luck
Right into the big combers.
You can't see where it goes.

And then it's waiting,
The bell on the rod whirring
In the gale, hands useless
In pockets, face frozen,

The white sea in the blackness
And some white stars
Between low cruising clouds
And the tide getting round you

And the rod-tip jerking
But only with the wind
With vibration from the breakers
Though the numb heart jumps.

Likely as not this is all
You'll ever get.
Likely as not this is all
You could ever stand.

THE SHRINE

Early in the morning they start to gather,
Drawn from the world of suffering to this place.
Languages collide and bruise each other
As buses and planes from all Europe and beyond
Arrive and unload their pathetic human freight.
Ash-white children with stick limbs, held by hefty

Sweating fathers, their eyes peering stupidly
From blankets, mingle with the not so bad—
The limpers with sticks and crutches; the half-paralysed;
Those with withered arms or knotted hands;
The deaf, the blind, the dumb, the idiots.
But worst are those in stretchers and wheelchairs,

Lined up as if to start a sprint at a school
Sports-day, wincing at the shock of the sun, some
Carrying dying flowers, some working rosaries
With white urgent fingers. What are they doing?
What does it mean, this gathering here each day
Where once somebody said she saw something?

MY MOTHER TONIGHT

In streets without children live the old,
And you among them. No human noise
Except for the gentle heeltaps of one or two
Out for their slow daily stroll or heading
For the grocery shop on the corner,
Admiring the flowers as they pass.

You are alone tonight
And every night, and all around you
Are others who are alone. Widows
Populate this place, quiet widows,
Though there are still a few men
Being nursed or pottering in the gardens.

It is a place of birds, their song
Riding over the old people,
Whose lives are lived out and concluded
To their bright clear music,
Soaring high, high and arching.
You watch them, feed them breadcrumbs,

Leave out and refill bowls of water,
For that is a way of feeling useful,
Like cutting back the grass, the flowers,
In this green and fertile landscape
Where growth seems to mock old lives.
You have nothing else to plant, to mould

To your ways. Nothing for all the long years.
You walk feather-light on life's surface,
Uninvolved now with anything of weight
Except grown children and memories.
Each day you wait for the mail, the phone—
Your lifelines in a barely moving sea.

In your mind it must be different.
There I know you still move far, still look
After people, have him there beside you.
There your footsteps are loud and strong,
Ringing the ground, turning heads.
But that is in your mind as you bend

To deadhead a flower, make some tea,
Talk kindly to a neighbour
About an illness or some new trouble.
The birds sing round you. I picture you tonight.
You are lonely in a street without children,
Old and alone, and your face is dear.

TEXAS BACKROADS, SUMMER

Here is inertia with no end.
The ground itself contains it, breathes it,
And an immensity of flatness
Stuns us like bereavement as we drive.
This since sun-up. All the hours, the heat.
We're lost.

There's a tall unpainted house
Back from the road, its old air full
Of sad couplings and slow dyings—
Such tiny human efforts out here
In the endless unwinding of our nightmare.
Or suddenly, windows smashed,
An abandoned concrete gas-station
With high-necked ethyl pumps and a wrecked pick-up.
Once some slow white-haired blacks
In underwear spitting on the ground as we passed.
Stopped, it's all silence, save for flies,
Dogs barking thin over miles,
A distant freight, a jacked-up Chevy

Full of kids in dungarees and billed hats
Giving us the finger, living their future
Right now, right here, in this land of dusty scrub.

We start again. Move faster. We are sinking
Too deeply inside ourselves. Our new map's useless.
From behind tilted windmills, weather-dented
Water-towers, that massive sun slides
Like hot oil down and across the windshield.
A long way out now, we're getting smaller.
We're leaving ourselves behind.
Slack, exhausted, totally unnerved,
We smell our own dust, and still the road goes on.

WILD BIRDS

for L.C.

Part of me
Thinks I should recognise them,
The eight or so different birds
Which have come to my tree today,
Or at least look them up
So I could put a name to them.

Some I've seen before.
Some I don't recognise,
The bright exciting ones with strange cries,
As if they'd stopped here for me,
Just for a moment, between continents
I've never been to or even heard of.
But I don't need to know.
I can't, after all, put names to all
The wings which beat inside me,
Those nightmare companions.

If they are to keep filling my dreams,
The restless wings, then I think
I'd be safer to be ignorant
As they whirr and clatter in my darkness,
Trying, trying to rise and soar,
Unable to lift my weight,
Trapped in my dead weight.

Through long nights they flit and crash
In my huge skull, my leaf and jungle skull,
As if trying to home somewhere,
To bring or send important messages,
But suddenly, in that hot lost place,
Baffled and confused, screaming,
Furiously beating,
Knowing that it shouldn't be this way,
That things are wrong and getting worse.

LEUTNANT STROBEL IS JUST ONE OF THEM

Always they bubble, loose, unexpected,
Erupting upwards for light, those images
We had thought forgotten, well tamped.

The remains of a German pilot killed
in the war have been found preserved
in marshland near Appledore, Kent.
His crashed Messerschmitt was close by.
An identity disc indicated he was probably
a Lt. Strobel, shot down on September 5, 1940,
in the Battle of Britain.

Right away we want more.
Did he carry photographs
Of a woman, children, parents, a house?
Or a well-creased letter—*Mein liebchen* . . . ?
Such things would help us find some comfort,
Like the way his plane stayed close to him
In the way of faithful dogs in legend.

The news release does add, tastefully,
Both the body and the pilot's clothing were
said by police to be in a remarkable condition.
But that's not enough, either,
For such a bizarre resurrection.
We have photographs of old bog-men.

The earth has gathered itself, drawn breath, stirred.
We can't leave this unattended to.
Leutnant Strobel is back among us
And will never be done with us,
Demanding, as such intrusions do,
Some kind of decent ceremony,
Our putting certain words for him
On paper and on stone.

Acknowledgements

GEORGE AMABILE: "Prairie," "Red River Wedding," "First Kill," "Misericordia General" and "Basilico" reprinted by permission of the author.
DOUGLAS BARBOUR: "Story for a Saskatchewan Night" and "two words / towards" by Douglas Barbour. Copyright © 1990 by Douglas Barbour. Reprinted by permission of Red Deer College Press. "Summer's Sea Son" and "Our Lady of the slowly freezing lakeshore—november:" from *shore lines* (Turnstone Press, 1979). © Douglas Barbour. Reprinted by permission. "song 19," "song 61," "song 64," "song 65," "song 89" and "breath ghazal number 11" reprinted by permission of the author.
E.D. BLODGETT: "weasel," "elephants" and "ursa major" reprinted by permission of the author. "for ducks," "Epistre dédicatoire (prologue)," "Leaving Louisbourg (N.S.)," "Métis," "Explorer" and "Pavanes." From *Da Capo: The Selected Poems of E.D. Blodgett*, 1990, NeWest Publishers Ltd. Reprinted by permission.
ELIZABETH BREWSTER: "On the death by burning of Kimberly Hammer, May 1972" reprinted by permission of the author. "Summers Here and There," "Map of the City," "Life Is a Flowing," "The Hero as Escape Artist," "The Living God," "Is the Pathetic Fallacy True?," "Metamorphosis" and "Each Journal an I-Land" are reprinted from *Selected Poems of Elizabeth Brewster* by permission of Oberon Press.
DENNIS COOLEY: "in his tangerine skin," "the end of the line," "freeze up," "the love song of j l krafchenko" and "by the red" from *Bloody Jack* (Turnstone Press, 1984). © Dennis Cooley. Reprinted by permission. "Jazz" by Dennis Cooley. Copyright © 1987 by Dennis Cooley. Reprinted by permission of Red Deer College Press. "prairie vernacular," "behind the door" and "trees in winter" were originally published in *Perishable Light* (Coteau Books, 1988). Reprinted with permission of the author and publisher. "Police Informer," by Dennis Cooley, from *Dedications* (Thistledown Press Ltd., 1988), used with permission. "gravity," "this only world" and "dried apricots" from *this only home* (Turnstone Press, 1992). © Dennis Cooley. Reprinted by permission.
LORNA CROZIER: "You're so covered with scars" from *No Longer Two People* (Turnstone Press, 1981), © Lorna Crozier. Reprinted by permission. "Marriage: Getting Used To," "The Fat Lady's Dance," "This One's for You," "The Foetus Dreams," "Drought," "Loon Song," "Cabbages," "Potatoes" and "Zucchini" from *The Garden Going on Without Us* by Lorna Crozier. Used by permission of the Canadian Publishers, McClelland & Stewart, Toronto. "The Oldest Song," "Without Hands," "Overture" and "Eggs" from *Angels of Flesh, Angels of Silence* by Lorna Crozier. Used by permisssion of the Canadian Publishers, McClelland & Stewart, Toronto. "On the Seventh Day" from *Inventing the Hawk* by Lorna Crozier. Used by permission of the Canadian Publishers, McClelland & Stewart, Toronto.
E.F. DYCK:"VI Mossbank: The Thirties" from *The Mossbank Canon* (Turnstone Press, 1982). © E.F. Dyck. Reprinted by permission. "S/HE," "At Stud" and "Experiments in Grammar" reprinted by permission of the author.
PATRICK FRIESEN: "curling at its edges," "my wife lies quietly" and "I wasn't thinking of the child" from *The Shunning* (Turnstone Press, 1980). © Patrick Friesen. Reprinted by

permission. "sunday afternoon," "wedding music" and "dream of the black river" from *Flicker and Hawk* (Turnstone Press, 1987). © Patrick Friesen. Reprinted by permission. "anna (first dance)" from *You Don't Get to Be a Saint* (Turnstone Press, 1992). © Patrick Friesen. Reprinted by permission. "terrain," "some kind of memory," "wings" and "summer going on fall" reprinted by permission of the author.

KRISTJANA GUNNARS: "straw hive," "dwarf pears" and "after shearing we washed" from *The Night Workers of Ragnarok* reprinted by permission of Beach Holme Publishing Limited. "changeling XVII," "monkshood XXVIII" and "Wakepick I" reprinted from *Wakepick Poems* by permission of House of Anansi Press. "dead," "slaughterhouse 2" and "blind 2" reprinted by permission of the author. "from memory V," "jóhann briem II," "jóhann briem IV" and "stéfan eyjólfsson XIV" from *Settlement Poems I* (Turnstone Press, 1980). © Kristjana Gunnars. Reprinted by permission. "Thorleifur Jóakimsson, Daybook II" from *Settlement Poems II* (Turnstone Press, 1980). © Kristjana Gunnars. Reprinted by permission.

JOHN V. HICKS: "Carol in Three-Three Time," "Reading Room," "Dark Morning," "The Talk of the Town" by John J. Hicks, from *Winter Your Sleep* (Thistledown Press Ltd., 1980), used with permission. "Night Flight," "Ursa Major," "Q.E.D.," "Frog on a Leash," "Full Moon," "You Know I Cannot Come" by John V. Hicks, from *Rootless Tree* (Thistledown Press Ltd., 1985), used with permission. "Do Not Disturb," "Keep Quite Still" and "Rubber Boot Boy" reprinted by permission of the author.

ROBERT KROETSCH: "The Silent Poet Sequence," "Mile Zero" and "Sounding the Name" from *Completed Field Notes* by Robert Kroetsch. Used by permission of the Canadian Publishers, McClelland & Stewart, Toronto.

ELI MANDEL: "Minotaur II," "City Park Merry-Go-Round," "Day of Atonement: Standing," "David," "Rapunzel," "Listen, the Sea," "Houdini," "Wabamun," "First Political Speech," "On the 25th Anniversary of the Liberation of Auschwitz," "from 'The Pentagon Papers,' " "birthmark," "estevan, 1934" and "returning from war" from *Dreaming Backwards,* reprinted by permission of Stoddart Publishing Co. Ltd. "Notes from the Underground," "In the Caves of My City," "The Gold Bug," "Hallowe'en by St. Mary's Convent," "Carleton University: January 1961," "The Comedians," "Psalm 24," "Reading Room: Periodicals," "the crooked gods" and "Going to Pieces" reprinted by permission of the Estate of Eli Mandel.

JOHN NEWLOVE: "What to Dream About" from *The Night the Dog Smiled* (ECW Press, 1986). Reprinted by permission. "Funeral," "In the Forest," "Susan 4," "Verigin III," "No Pleasure," "Last Summer a Number of Our People Died Just for a Want of Something to Live On," "My Daddy Drowned," "Not Moving," "The Singing Head," "Verigin, Moving in Alone," "Ride off Any Horizon," "Indian Women," "Public Library," "The Prairie" and "The Cave" reprinted by permission of the author.

GLEN SORESTAD: "(at batoche, june 1975)," "Homestead," "Shitepoke," "Beginnings" and "Knives and Fish" reprinted by permission of the author. "Alexandra," "Backyard Moment" and "Shelling Peas" by Glen Sorestad were originally published in *Hold the Rain in Your Hands: Poems New and Selected* (Coteau Books, 1985). Reprinted with permission of the author and publisher. "Early Morning Sun" and "The Amateur Gardener" by Glen Sorestad, from *West into Night* (Thistledown Press Ltd., 1991), used with permission. "Amsterdam Dog Walker" from *Air Canada Owls* (Harbour Publishing, 1990), reprinted by permission.

ANDREW SUKNASKI: "Overland to the Southern Plain," "Love within Shadows," "the robson street waitress," "Jimmy Hoy's Place," "Koonohple," "Letters between Two Prairie Friends," "Leaving Home Again," "Registration of Death," "To Whom It May Concern" and "Manhattan Borscht" reprinted by permission of the author.

ANNE SZUMIGALSKI: "Angels" first published in *A Game of Angels* (Turnstone Press), "The Arrangement," "Shrapnel" and "The Bees" first published in *Doctrine of Signatures* (Fifth House), and "Looking for Uncle Tich" first published in *Dogstones* (Fifth House), reprinted by permission of Anne Szumigalski. "On Singleness" and "On the Sun" by Anne Szumigalski. Copyright © 1985 by Anne Szumigalski. Reprinted by permission of Red Deer College Press. "Halinka," "The Flight" and "The Boy at the Upstairs Window with His Head in His Hands" by Anne Szumigalski were originally published in *Rapture of the Deep* (Coteau Books, 1991). Reprinted with permission of the author and publisher.
JON WHYTE: "Magot Pie," "More or Less," "Ruddy and Masked Ducks" and "Learning the world spins" reprinted by permission of the Estate of Jon Whyte.
CHRISTOPHER WISEMAN: "The Deaf-Mute," "Prayer for My Children," "The Sphinx Wasp," "Barbarian Remembers and Loves His Children," "The Question," "Flamborough Head," "Cod Fishing," "The Shrine" and "My Mother Tonight," from *Post Cards Home* (Sono Nis Press, 1988), reprinted by permission. "Texas Backroads, Summer," "Wild Birds" and "Leutnant Strobel Is Just One of Them" from *Missing Persons* (Sono Nis Press, 1989), reprinted by permission.

Recent Poetry by Turnstone Press

this only home by Dennis Cooley

You Don't Get to Be a Saint by Patrick Friesen

saving face by Roy Miki

standing all the night through by Audrey Poetker

Something to Madden the Moon by Brenda Riches

Without Benefit of Words by Kathleen Wall